Bass R

LAWMAN

Book two of the Bass Reeves trilogy

FRED STAFF

Dedication

The Bass Reeves Series is dedicated to:

Royce Peterson, retired Professor of History at the University of Central Oklahoma;
Jack Scammahorn, my longtime friend and fellow teacher;
Bob Brousseau, my wise old friend who has encouraged me strongly in all aspects
of life's journey;
Dennis Hambright, who has continually encouraged me in my writing efforts; and
Gypsy Hogan, who has been a tremendous encouragement to me
and of great assistance to this project.

Foreword

This is the second part of the Bass Reeves trilogy. It will take Bass from his entry into the U.S. Marshal's service through his great exploits as the most feared lawman of his times. Readers will find themselves riding with a determined and dedicated man, whose only motivation is to see justice done, no matter whether it is personal or in the enforcement of federal law.

As you travel with Bass Reeves, you will face more challenges and find that survival is based on your ability to out-smart, out-ride and out-shoot more desperate men than is imaginable.

Indian Territory was without a doubt the most violent and untamed area in the United States during the times of Bass Reeves, and it was only through his and other marshals' efforts that peace and statehood was accomplished.

The history of the Old West is filled with stories of heroes and villains, and those stories have been a source of fascination for generations. The fact that the stories of these unique and colorful characters continue to intrigue people all over the world is a true testament to the grit and determination it actually took to tame a wild and unpredictable country.

Among those stories, readers will seldom find a character that overcame more challenges and had more determination than Bass Reeves. Reeves was born a slave and served a man who ultimately became the Speaker of the House of Texas. He was a participant in the Civil War and escaped his life of slavery by fleeing to the lawless Indian Territory, now part of Oklahoma.

Bass Reeves faced challenges in his new homeland that would have destroyed a lesser man, but his natural gifts of determination and intelligence helped mold the man into one of the most feared and respected lawmen in history.

The story of Bass Reeves was illuminated in his day by only a flicker of candlelight, because he was black. If he had been a white man, the entire world would have known of his great exploits, and his name would have been mentioned with the likes of Wyatt Earp, Bat Masterson and Bill Hickok. If the real truth had been known, the name of Bass Reeves would have been a beacon of historical light, shining brighter than any of his contemporaries.

The truth is, many of those more famous lawmen also reveled in some of the less honorable sides of life, like gambling, prostitution, profiteering, murder and vengeance. To the contrary, research into the life of Bass Reeves has shown that he strictly obeyed the laws of the land and strove to treat the men he hunted with even more respect than was customary for that time in history. Amazingly, Reeves stuck to these high standards in a wild territory that was often filled with greater danger than any of his contemporaries could have imagined.

Bass Reeves brought law to a territory of outlaws that spread over seventy thousand square miles. He arrested more than three-thousand offenders and delivered them to face judgment before Judge Parker, known as the hanging judge in Fort Smith, Arkansas. During the time Reeves brought justice to his territory, records show that in one violent year alone, there were ten thousand murders in the entire United States, and three thousand of those heinous acts were committed within Reeves' jurisdiction. In the entire history of the U.S. Marshal Service, two hundred marshals were killed, with one hundred and twenty of those occurring in Indian Territory.

The details of this story are based on a tremendous amount of research, and I'd like to thank Art Burton, author of Black, Red and Deadly, and Black Gun, Silver Star, for his dedicated research, helping to shine a long-deserved light on Bass Reeves, a true American hero.

Chapter 1

Changes

Time had allowed Sam and Bass to accomplish the arduous task of cleaning and repairing the house, damages left by the outlaws who had killed their good friend, kidnapped Sam's wife and children, and sent the two men on a deadly chase of rescue, where they had lost still another brave friend.

Sam and Bass would never forget the sacrifice their friend Charley had made in trying to defend the home and family while the two men were away. The fight to save those at home not only had claimed Charley's life, but it had nearly destroyed the interior of the house as gunfire had shattered wood and glass. Charley's blood had so stained the floor that the planks had to be replaced.

Even though the home now looked as good as it ever had, the memories that it contained made living there a challenge. The children seemed to have withstood the trauma and dealt with the aftermath of the ordeal. Lidia, in her staunch commitment to make the family's life first-rate, seemed to have washed the tragic events from her mind.

Nonetheless, they all were more cautious when visitors approached, as they were the evening when Bass was bringing an armload of firewood to the house and noticed riders coming down the trail at full gallop.

The family was relieved somewhat when the riders let out the familiar Cherokee cry that indicated theirs was a friendly approach. The cry seemed to have an extra ring, as the riders knew they were entering a space that had suffered greatly, and that the men of the house were in no condition with which to be trifled.

The riders slowed as they approached, and, in the evening sun, it still was possible to determine that they were members of the Light Horse patrol. They pulled their ponies to a halt and calmly walked them to the corral.

Sam and Bass walked to the corral and greeted them. The riders spoke in Cherokee, apologizing and explaining that although they knew the family was on edge, they had hurried down the trail to get there before nightfall so they could be recognized as friendly. They certainly did not want to face the guns of Bass and Sam.

In the conversation, the Light Horsemen all expressed their sorrow for the horrible events that had taken place and apologized for not having been closer in the family's time of need. All in the group knew that the events would have been totally different if the patrol had been in the area.

John Pullum, the leader of the group, finally spoke. "I know you had great stress, and we all hate the loss of Charley, but we've come with some comfortin' news. It seems that after we gathered the bodies and sent the identification to Fort Smith, that each and every one of the skunks had a price on 'is head. The total for the twelve killed comes to two thousand, seven hundred and fifty dollars."

Bass and Sam stood silent for a moment. They looked at each other, both in deep thought and knowing what the other was thinking. Their silence was not broken for several minutes. Each man was trying to assess the value of John's words. The loss of trusted friends had no price, they both knew. It especially haunted Sam that his friend Walter had sacrificed his life, Walter who had served in the war with Sam, but was not even a Cherokee brother.

Sam finally broke the silence and asked, "What was the price on the man that Walter killed?"

"Which one did he kill?" the Light Horseman named John asked.

"The one with the knife wound, and one of those in the meadow," Sam said.

"Let me check the paper work."

John walked to his saddlebag and pulled out a thick stack of papers. He slowly went through them before replying, "It seems that the fellow with a stab wound had a two hundred and fifty dollar price on his head, and the one in the meadow had one hundred and fifty."

"OK, now what was the price on the one with all the .22 holes in 'im? That's the one that Little Sam killed," Sam said, inquiring on behalf of his young son.

Again, John fumbled through the stack, and, holding the papers close to his face and at an angle to catch the fading light, he said, "He had a three hundred and fifty dollar bill, dead or alive, on him."

"What about the two bastards Charley got here in the yard with the shotgun wounds?" Sam asked.

John strained to read his paper and finally asked, "Could we go in the house? There's not enough light to finish all this readin'."

Suddenly embarrassed by his lack of hospitality, Sam quickly said, "Sure, sorry for not askin' you in earlier. I was so taken back by the news that I wasn't thinkin'. All of you come in, and Lidia will make some coffee. You probably could use it 'bout now."

Once in the house, the group found seats, while John again began to shuffle through the papers before finally saying, "They each had two hundred dollars on 'em. You know, all of those critters were a sore on the ass of humanity, and you two really did a nice job of cleanin' up some of the troubles here 'bouts."

Sam said, "Well, we did some of it, but others deserve credit, and I aim to see that their survivors share in the reward. What do you say Bass?"

Bass stroked his mustache and added, "None of this would've come out like it did if it weren't for all of us. They sure get my vote for their fair share."

John reached into his saddlebag and produced a stack of bills, placed them on the table and said, "All you've got to do is sign each paper, and this is yours."

Sam stepped forward and put his signature on each of the papers. Then Bass took each paper and examined it. He saw where Sam had signed, then marked his "X" underneath Sam's handwriting.

Business out of the way, John and the other members of the patrol shook hands with the two men, returned to the hot coffee. They grasped the cups firmly with both hands and held the cup close to their face to feel the warmth and enjoy the aroma.

While they drank, small talk was abundant. Most of these men had known Sam all of his life, and the reputation that Bass had made for himself made him an honored member of the group of lawmen. They spoke of Charley, how tough he had been, noting that of all the members of the Light Horse, Charley was the man they each would have chosen to protect their own family.

Later, Sam asked, "Why don't you fellows sleep in the barn tonight? It looks like it might be a little chilly out, and I sure wouldn't want you to catch a sickness after doin' what you've done. That wind can be piercing. If you do, Lidia will fix you some pancakes in the mornin'."

John said, "I need to get back to the wife, but some of us might stay."

The others all said they, too, needed to go. None of them wanted to be away from home more than necessary. They were the men who protected the Cherokee homeland, so they knew too well that there were men everywhere just looking for an easy mark. While they all said they would enjoy some of Lidia's pancakes, they thought it too big a gamble. This lawless land could not allow any of them such a simple pleasure.

Their departure was swift and friendly. As they left the yard, Sam, already with a plan of action, turned to Bass and said, "We've a lot to do in the next few days. I'd like you to go to the Seminole village where Walter lived and give his money to his wife. She sure could use it. It should take you about two days. I'll stay here with the family 'til you get back, and then I'll take Charley's share of the money to Sally. I know she wasn't his wife, but he spoke so much of her, and he has no family."

"If you tell me the way, I'll be goin' at sun up," Bass said.

"No problem. I'll draw you a map," Sam said.

***

When the morning sun crested the ridge above the house, Bass was already dressed. With his bedroll under his arm, he took one last drink of coffee and headed for the door.

The wind had a chill in it, causing him to pull his collar up around his ears. His horse, King, was waiting and appeared to be ready for an outing. Bass saddled King, and then mounted. He walked the horse past the corral gate before putting the huge horse into a slow gallop.

Soon the sun was bearing down, helping to offset the chill. Bass was glad that he was headed south and not having to face the crisp, north wind.

He recalled first coming to this land, after his escape from slavery during the battle of Pea Ridge, how both the weather and the lay of the land had struck him as so different from what he had known. Master Reeves' farm was much flatter, and the weather never seemed to be this cold in northeast Texas. Nonetheless, Bass was glad that he was no longer a slave, no matter how kindly Master Reeves had treated him.

Sam's map was clear, made easier by the fact that Bass had traveled the major part of the route on an earlier trip. King's long strides allowed them to make excellent time, and, about noon, Bass pulled up to have some jerky and biscuits. He took long drinks from his canteen, then walked to a sun-soaked rock and sat for a while studying the land. He always was looking for points to guide him in the future, knowledge that might serve him well.

This was the first time that he had been alone since the murder of Charley and the kidnapping of Sam's family. As Bass tried to relax, flashes of the tremendous chase and the ultimate killing of those bastards came back to mind. Bass saw their deaths as being caused by their own insane actions. He hoped that he would never again face circumstances like those, but he had no doubt that he would shoot and kill again if needed.

Bass then began to think of Little Sam and how brave he had been. Even now, Bass was amazed at how the young boy had remained strong. With a broken arm, having just faced death and having killed the man who killed Charley, Little Sam's first thoughts had been about the well being of his little sister, Sarah. The boy's actions made Bass love and respect him even more.

At last, Bass shook his head and tried to clear all these thoughts from his mind. The one thing that he knew would bring him back to the present was to get his mind back to the lay of the land and the appreciation of nature.

Turning from side to side, taking in all that was around him was just a part of his life. Suddenly, out of the corner of his eye, he saw a quick flash in the trees about fifty feet above the trail. This reflection was out of place and could only be taken as a warning.

Someone was in those trees, and while they might be harmless, Bass could not take a chance. People who did not take precautions in this country soon found themselves in an abundance of trouble.

Bass quickly left the rock and walked down the slight grade to King. He pulled the Spencer from the boot, and with the cover of the rocks, he scurried up the side of the hill, blending into the trees. He cautiously maneuvered above the spot where he had seen the flash. He moved quickly, but silently, to a position above and somewhat behind the point. Then he squatted, looked and listened.

The survival skills Sam had taught him started to work. He turned his eyes from side to side and paid attention to the birds in the trees. Just as he had suspected, there were no birds in the trees and none landing in the area he was observing. Time now was his ally. White men can't sit still, and if there was someone there, he would soon show himself.

Bass' wait was short. A man with a rifle in his hand slowly stood up and stepped a little forward, looking directly at where Bass had been sitting. In a moment, another man with a rifle took a position beside him. They both were crouched and appeared to be whispering to each other. As they surveyed the area, Bass slipped even further behind them and carefully started to descend the hill.

He soon spotted the men's horses, and then made his way carefully past them. In seconds, he was within easy range of the two men as they stretched on the ground with their rifles trained on the trail.

Bass took a few more steps toward them, and then raised his rifle to his shoulder.

"You boys lookin' for me?"

The two jumped as if he had fired a round at them. They started to swing toward the voice with their rifles in their hands when Bass shouted, "Don't move an inch, 'cause that inch 'ill get you six feet of dirt!"

The two men's good fortune was that they did not continue to turn.

"Now lay your rifles down slowly and undo your belts, slowly, and let 'em fall to the ground." Bass' deep and firm voice had truly made an impression on the bushwhackers. They each glanced at the other, while carefully following Bass' instructions. Bass then said, "Now put your hands on top of your heads and try not to breathe too deep. I might think you're up to somethin' and have to put a bullet in your ear. Don't turn my way. Now sit on that rock and take your boots off. If you turn, I'll drop you."

As the men were starting to sit, Bass fired a round and took the hat off the head of one of the men.

"I'm sorry, boys. It's just that sometimes I let go one of these rounds, and sometimes I never know when that'll be. Now hurry before that urge hits me again."

The bushwhackers sat down quickly and furiously took off their boots.

"Now, you see that big rock over there about two hundred yards?" Bass asked.

He then fired another round, drawing dust from the rock.

"That was just in case you couldn't figure it out. Now, you'd better make dust toward it or another one of these rounds might just put more than one hole in your backside."

The two started down the hill, rushing as best they could, but continually hollering and shouting as their bare feet stepped on rocks, twigs and other types of sharp objects. When they hit the open area by the trail, they increased their flight, except once in a while they stumbled and jumped from the sharp impact to their feet, from time to time bending down and removing objects stuck in their tender flesh.

A huge smile crossed Bass' face as he watched the two men try to run. They were now without boots, guns and horses. They would have to make it on their own. If they were lucky, they would make it to someone's house. If not, they had made a choice and would have to pay the price. Bass hoped they would take this lesson to heart, but knew that he may face them again one day, as Indian Territory was the home, harbor and breeding grounds for those who thrived on lawlessness.

Bass gathered their articles and went back up the hill, untied the horses, mounted one of them and led the other back to King. He tethered them together and led them off on his journey to the village. After a few hundred yards, he threw the boots in the brush. They were in such bad condition that there was no salvage value in them.

He kept smiling as he rode. Recalling the site of the two was the most fun he had had in a long time. He, again, hoped the men had learned their lesson and would give up their ways. If nothing else, their sore feet should keep them out of trouble for a while.

Bass got to the village just at dusk and was greeted by a pack of barking and yelping dogs. While the dogs were running around the horses, a man stepped out with a rifle and said, "Who is you, and what is you doin' here?"

Bass was momentarily shocked by the fact that the man was black. Bass recalled that many of the tribes had taken their slaves in as equals. The fact that he also had been a recipient of this tradition made it more understandable.

With his hands somewhat raised, Bass said, "I am Bass Reeves, and I have come to bring somethin' to Walter Upton's wife. I mean no harm and have come as a friend."

After a short pause, the man said, "I've heard of yah. Follow me, and I'll take yah to 'er place."

As they moved through the village, other members of the tribe came out to see what kind of person would be entering their village at this time of day. They all stood and stared. Some of the children ran beside Bass and King. The children were amazed at the size of the animal, and the man riding him. They looked at the revolvers hanging from Bass' side, and immediately realized that this was a man of action. The combination of horse and rider made a sight that none had ever seen and probably would not see again.

In the middle of the village, the man motioned for Bass to stop before a shack that had a big deer hide for a door. The shack was not that much different than the others, but there was a feeling about it, something that told of the emptiness inside.

Bass was motioned in, so he dismounted, went to his pack and withdrew a sack. He walked to the house, removing his hat as he entered.

The black man introduced Bass to Irma Upton. She nodded her head and motioned for Bass to sit down.

Bass studied her for several minutes, while she was doing the same of him.

She obviously was older than Bass, and her faced exhibited stress and worry. Her dress was disheveled, and her hair was unkempt, but as Bass appraised her, he could see a woman of beauty under all of the outward signs of pain.

What seemed like an hour really was only several minutes. Bass finally spoke, holding his hat over his chest. "I've come here to bring you somethin'."

He immediately realized she had no idea what he was saying. So in Creek he repeated the statement.

The look on her face showed that she understood, so he continued in Creek.

"I have some money for you. It is not a gift. Walter earned it. I also want to share your sorrow. Without Walter's help, I would have suffered the loss of three people I hold dear in my heart. He was a brave man, and I honor him, not only with the money I have brought, but I have two horses and several weapons I wish to give to you with my great gratitude."

In the middle of his statement, the hide covering the back room of the house slowly folded back, and a young lady stepped out. Even in the dim light of the room, it was evident that she was beautiful. Her hair was raven black, and her large brown eyes danced in the flickering light. Her skin was smooth, and the high cheekbones were a perfect complement to her well-shaped nose and thin lips.

"I'm sorry for interruptin'. I'm Walter's daughter, Jane. I speak some English and Creek, and, of course, Seminole. I heard you talkin' and I'd like to help. My mother appreciates the fact that you've taken the time to come to us with kind words and money. It'll sure be needed. She'd like for you to stay and share our food and talk of my father."

Bass was unable to move for a moment. He had been in many a fight, but he had never been spellbound until now. After collecting himself, he said, "I'd be more'n happy to share with you, but I must tell you that I know nothin' of your father. We only met for a few seconds. I can tell you of his unselfish deeds and his bravery, but nothin' else."

Jane said, "That's not important. My mother will speak of him, and I will interpret. The things you wish to add, I'll happily share with her. It is our custom to speak of the dead. It helps them on their trip. Your listenin' makes his path easier."

The meager meal was served, and they sat for hours. Bass mostly listened to Jane, and the more he listened, the more intrigued he became with her. Jane smiled at times, a smile that was magical. She shed tears while exhibiting a strength that was impressive. The longer Bass looked into her eyes, the more taken he was with her.

Except for the time as a boy when he had pulled two drowning girls from a creek, looking at a woman had been something that he had continually kept out of his mind. This was an experience he had never faced, and he totally did not know how to react. He felt as awkward as he had when he ate his first meal with Master Reeves. He did not know what or how to do anything at the moment.

Late into the night, Jane said, "It's time for bed." She reached for his hand and led him back through the deer hide door. Once inside, she turned toward him and kissed him, then slowly undressed him. She led him to her bed, and said, "Here is where we will stay."

Chapter 2

The New Life

The next morning was the beginning of a new life and world for Bass. He had never before experienced the touch and warmth of a woman, and he was totally confused. The only thing that came to his mind was the conversations he had overheard as a boy listening to Master Reeves and his friends gathered on the Reeves' porch. Bass now had some understanding of what the men had been talking about when they spoke of women and the great enjoyment they got from them.

He rose, dressed and entered the small dining area of the humble home where he was greeted with a broad smile from Jane. She was busying herself with preparation for breakfast and coffee. She did not speak, but scurried about the kitchen.

Bass stood and could not take his eyes from her. Just the vision of her working in the tiny kitchen brought thoughts to his mind of home and peace. These things had been so far from his mind only hours before that he was stunned that they even existed in him.

Jane turned as she placed the cup of coffee on the table and said, "You sleep well?"

Bass was speechless for a moment. Then a broad smile covered his face as he replied, "Yes, very well, thank you."

"Sit and have coffee. I'll have you some food in a moment."

Bass did as instructed. Before he had finished his coffee, he was greeted with a plate of eggs and fried bread.

With a warm smile Jane said, "Eat, you may need the strength."

Bass picked up the fork and, using the fried bread as a guide, started consuming the offering.

Jane took a seat opposite him and said, "Bass, my family doesn't need me here. It's just one more mouth to feed, and times are hard. I don't see them gettin' any better. I was wonderin' if you'd take me with you?"

The egg that Bass had just attempted to put in his mouth fell back into his plate. He looked up and was speechless for a moment, then said in a very slow voice, "Miss, you don't know me, and I hardly know you."

With a smile on her face, Jane said, "I tried to introduce myself as best I could last night, and I know you from the stories I've heard. This land is large, but stories of brave men travel fast, and yours has crossed many lips. I'll try to keep you happy best I can, and if I don't, I'll try to find someplace else."

"I don't know what you think you're gettin' into. You should remember that stories are just stories — don't mean they is true. Besides, I live in a one-room shed that we attached to the barn, and I spend my time workin' horses and in the field. Nothin' special 'bout that."

"I guess you think there's somethin' special 'bout this? Listen, I promise you I can make you happy and that there's no woman that can work harder than me. Again, if I can't, I'll leave."

Bass sat in silence. He was in deep thought, but these thoughts kept going back to the night before. He slowly took a bit of the fried bread and reinserted the egg in his mouth, never taking his eyes off of Jane.

Jane simply sat and looked him in the eyes, with a warm and inviting smile on her face.

Bass took a long and slow drink from his cup, set it down and asked, "How much stuff you got?"

Like a hummingbird, Jane darted around the table and threw her arms around Bass' neck. She placed her warm lips on Bass' still filled mouth. She held them there for a few moments before breaking away and rushing toward the back room.

Bass' thoughts of what he had done were interrupted by noises coming from the back room. Before he could totally come to his senses, Jane emerged with a carpetbag in her hand and a pair of shoes tied together by the laces drooped over her arm.

Bass stared at the baggage, but could not help but look up into the eyes of this beautiful woman. She was young and full of life, and when you matched that with her aggressiveness, he could not think of anything that should keep him from keeping his earlier commitment.

Bass sat for a moment before reaching into his pocket and pulling out his poke. He counted out fifty dollars and slid it across the table toward Jane.

She looked at it for a moment as hurt began to cross her face and she started to say something hostile to him. Fortunately, before she could get it out, Bass said, "Give that to your mother. I am taking the mare I brought to 'er last night, and this should be more 'nuff to cover the cost. Now go and say your goodbyes and I'll get the horses ready."

By the time Jane came out through the deerskin door, Bass had the horses saddled and Jane's carpetbag attached behind the mare.

Jane looked for a moment before rushing to Bass. She had to stand on her tiptoes to reach her arms around his neck, but managed to pull him over and placed another warm kiss on his lips. She then pulled herself away and athletically jumped into the awaiting saddle.

"Come on, what're you waitin' for? I'm gonna make you very happy, and I'm ready to go," she said with a laugh.

Bass pushed his hat back on his head and stumbled toward King. For some reason he felt clumsier than he ever had.

The trip back to the Mankiller farm was filled with thoughts and plans. What was he going to do with this woman? How were Sam and the rest going to react to an addition to the farm? Was she for real or was this just some kind of a dream that had manifested itself?

By looking at his companion, he knew that she was for real, and the longer he observed her grace in the saddle, the more he was convinced that she could be a valuable addition to the partnership. She rode with ease, and she appeared to have more confidence in where she was going and what she could do than about any lady he had ever observed.

Bass finally decided that Jane would be a good match for Lidia and that the two had many similar characteristics. He hoped that the children would take to her, thinking that they would be the ultimate test for her acceptance.

Bass concluded that all things happen for a purpose and that if you give situations time, they will work the way they are supposed to work. This may be one more occurrence when he should just to sit back and let things develop.

Chapter 3

Unbelievable

Bass and Jane made an uneventful journey to the Mankiller homestead, arriving about sundown.

Looking down on the home made a beautiful setting. The sun made the newly painted house dance as the shadows from the surrounding trees swayed across its surface. The corral was full of fine looking horses, and the new addition to the barn showed that there was more prosperity in the valley.

Jane pulled her mare to a halt as they topped the ridge and stood in her saddle. She stared intently at the welcoming valley before sitting back in the saddle and turning to Bass to ask, "Is this it?"

Bass nodded yes, then smiled as he realized that it was more than she had expected. Her reaction sparked a feeling of pride in him. He only then realized how many positive changes had taken place in the once stark valley.

Bass descended toward the valley floor and gave out the customary shout of arrival. The house responded as usual. This time the children were much bigger than his first arrival, and they ran much faster and hooped and hollered their greetings to the man to whom they now were so attached.

By the time Bass and Jane had reached the valley floor, the children were already around the corner of the corral. They slowed their gait as they realized that Bass was not alone. They strained their eyes to make out who was accompanying him.

As Bass and his new companion got closer, the children stopped completely and waited for the pair to approach. Their smiles were still prevalent on their faces, but the inquisitive look increased with each step of the horses.

Instead of standing to greet the couple, both children turned and raced for the front porch, where their parents stood with their arms interlocked. They rushed onto the porch and took positions on either side of their parents.

Now all four stood and analyzed the couple approaching. As the pair passed the corral and turned toward the house, Sam stepped down the steps and slowly approached.

"Looks like you picked up some baggage on the trail," Sam said good-naturedly.

A smile so wide that it showed his teeth under his mustache traversed Bass' face as he tipped his hat back on his head.

"Well, it's not baggage. I have brought a friend. This is Jane, Walter's daughter."

"Now that I'm closer, I can see that, and a mighty pretty friend I might add," Sam said, grinning.

"Well, she might actually be more than a friend. Sam, if it is OK, Miss Jane will probably be stayin' a while," Bass said tentatively.

Sam smiled and said, "Whatever pleases you just makes my day, but you'll have to get the blessin's of the two boss ladies. I doubt, though, that'll be any problem. Besides, it might keep you from bein' so cranky."

Sam let out a big laugh and slapped his leg before taking the reins of both horses and leading them toward the house.

Bass smiled and looked toward Jane. He observed a small smile appearing on her thin lips.

When they got to the porch, Sam dropped the reins and took a deep bow. He then stepped toward the porch, turned sideways and pointed his hand toward the pair, saying, "May I present the honorable Bass Reeves and his companion and bed warmer, Miss Jane."

Jane smiled, but even her dark skin was evidently turning a darker shade. She dropped her head a little as she raised her hand in greeting and in Cherokee said, "Hello, I am pleased to be here, and I hope that you will accept me as a friend and fellow worker."

Lidia stepped forward and said, "You are more than welcome here. If Bass speaks well of you and you are the daughter of the man that saved my husband's life, there is no need for more discussion."

***

In a very short time, Jane earned the respect of the Mankiller family. She was an excellent help in the kitchen, and her work in the field was on an equal with any member of the family. She was exceedingly effective in working with the horses, which of course, made Bass exceptionally proud. The horses responded well to her, and she showed a sense of understanding that enabled her to recognize the individual personalities of each ward and use it in their training.

The mare's colt was now getting into his second year and her fondness for him was evident. She personally broke him the Indian way by constantly being around him, daily rubbing his back with a blanket and ever so slowly applying more and more weight. When the day came, all she had to do was place a saddle on him and mount the now magnificent young stud.

The first day she laid eyes on him, she had named him for the great white streak that covered his now distinguished face. Blaze seemed to be the only fitting name for her charge, and the entire group approved. It turned out that Sarah also had that name in mind for him, but had never expressed herself. When the name was discussed at the supper table, the young girl became overly excited with approval.

It had been a particularly mild winter, and with spring approaching, the valley was coming to life more rapidly than usual. Spring chores were starting, and each had their duties. Of course, the most important chores for the children were to first get their schoolwork done.

With the warming spring days also came the much welcome rains. During a usual downpour, Bass and Sam were sitting on the front porch waiting for a break in the rain when they observed a man, with his hat pulled down on his head and covered by a slicker, slowly heading his horse down the trail toward the house.

They took their usual precautions, even though they sensed that the gait and actions of the rider made it unlikely that alarm was warranted.

As he approached, he raised both hands in a sign of peace and looked toward the two men. In spite of the hat riding low on his face, and the water dripping from the brim, Sam recognized him.

"Johnny, what are you doing? Get in here and out of the rain," Sam said with a smile on his face.

The man slowly dismounted and tied his horse to the tree next to the house. Even though the rain was falling by the buckets, he took his time approaching the porch.

Sam stood and offered his hand. When Johnny took it, Sam pulled him rapidly to the shelter of the overhang.

"Johnny, I haven't seen you since the battle of Pea Ridge. How've you been?"

As Johnny took his hat from his head and slapped it against his leg, he kept his eyes directed toward the porch floor.

"Well, Sam, they've not been good. That's why I'm here. Of all the people I know, you're the only one that I felt I could trust."

With a look of concern, Sam said, "I appreciate that, but what do you need from me? You know if I can do it, I will."

With a look of sadness on his face and his shoulders drooping, he said, "It's simple. Tomorrow I will die."

Sam said, "I told you to stop that drinkin' — it's givin' you crazy notions. Now what's the real problem?"

"True, the drinkin' was the start of the problem, but I'm serious about tomorrow. 'Bout a year ago, when I was drinkin' with the brothers, they started tellin' me that my wife was sleepin' with a Creek. I drank more and finally went home to beat the truth out of my wife, and when I did, I kilt 'er. I went and found the bastard and ended up stabbin' 'im to death. Later, it was learned that it was my wife's sister who had been sleepin' with the Creek. She looked so much like my wife that people got 'em confused. I just didn't take the time to think."

"My God man, that is terrible."

"Well, the Cherokee court sentenced me to die tomorrow, but since I had three little babies, they let me go home and see them through the winter. They gave me time to get 'em placed with other people and sell my farm so they could have some money. The court didn't want to put any more problems on 'em than necessary.

"I got all of that done, and I just have one more thing I need to do. I's wonderin' if you'd come in tomorrow and make sure my horse gets sold and the kids get the money? I'd really like it if'n you'd be there when they shoot me. I'd like to have a friend close by."

Sam stood with his mouth open. He slowly turned his gaze from Johnny to Bass. Sam was speechless, as was Bass.

The silence that filled the porch was interrupted only by the sound of the rain on the roof. The claps of thunder seemed to make even more dramatic the unbelievable revelation that the two men had just heard.

Sam after a few minutes of thought, said, "Johnny, Johnny. I can't believe my ears. You and I've been through so much together. You know I'll do anythin' I can, but I'm havin' one hell of a time gettin' round this."

After a pause, Sam added, "Is there nothin' that can be done?"

"No, I done it, and I's wrong. The court treated me real good, and I need to do my part. I'm at peace. My kids are settled, and it's my duty to leave 'em knowin' I still have bravery and honor."

"Well, no one ever worried about your bravery, or your honor," Sam said. "I can remember when we used to count coup on the Seminole and Creek, there was no one braver than you. In the battles in the war, you were the one that I could always count on."

Sam stared at the floor for a moment and shook his head.

"I'll be there for you, don't worry 'bout that," he finally said.

The rain suddenly stopped, and moments later, the sun broke through the clouds and bathed the valley with welcomed warmth.

Johnny took his slicker off and shook the rain out, then turned to the two and said, "I take that as a sign. All will be well. Your promise to me has made this a great day, and I think tomorrow will be a great day to die."

He stuck his hand out and took Sam's hand. They both pulled together and patted each other warmly on the back.

Sam said, "Go with peace. I'll do what I promised."

"I know that's why I picked you," Johnny said.

He turned and mounted. His gait seemed to be lighter and faster as he headed toward town.

Bass and Sam stood silently on the porch as they watched Johnny disappear.

"That is the most unbelievable thing I think I've ever seen or heard," Bass finally said. "You're really goin' ain't you?"

"As much as I hate to, I promised and I will," Sam said. "We may as well go over to the Ross'. I know they'll be goin'. Our families can travel together, so at least we can have some fellowship on this gloomy day."

Chapter 4

The Day

The next day, the household rose early and traveled the three miles to the Ross homestead. The day was somewhat brisk, as many early spring days tend to be. However, as the sun got higher in the sky, pleasing warmth accompanied the group in their travel.

Little Sam was riding his new pony. Unable to control his excitement, the young boy rode ahead several times before returning at full speed. His delight in having a mount of his own was more than evident.

The remainder of the group moved at a reasonable pace and, in short time, approached the Ross' valley. As they approached, Sam released the usual greetings, and soon the little house was abuzz with children, dogs and even a cat that ran from the house to the barn.

The barking dogs met Sam's group first and continued to escort them down the trail, barking and sometimes snapping at the horses as they advanced. Their noise and constant harassment of the horses was unwelcome, but a common thing in these parts of the country. All of the horses handled it well except for Little Sam's paint pony, which seemed to take great exception to the unrelenting pestering.

Little Sam had to hold tight to his pony, and it appeared that the more the pony kicked and leaped, the more the dogs enjoyed their action. Finally, the pony landed a lucky shot with his kick and lifted a menacing dog several feet in the air. The previous noise from the dogs could not compare to the screech of pain released by the victim. The others took their lesson from the event, placing their tails between their legs and scampering toward the safety of the house.

The Ross' greeted their neighbors and invited them in for some coffee. The beverage was welcome and the chance for some moments of peace and quiet was greatly appreciated. After some polite exchanges, Sam said, "I hate to cut this short, but I've got to get to town before noon. Maybe we could continue the visit in the saddle?"

John Ross said, "I've a better idea. I hitched the team to the wagon, and the ladies can ride there and visit all they want, while the men ride beside. I need to take the wagon anyways. We need supplies, and it would be more comfortable for the women."

"Sounds fine to me. How 'bout it ladies?" Sam asked.

They all shook their heads in agreement, picking up their coats and hats as they departed to the wagon.

As the entourage got closer to Tahlequah, the movement of people on the road became far more than usual. There were riders in ones and twos with others in groups of ten, as well as an abundance of all types of wheeled carts heading toward town.

Sam said, "You don't suppose all of these people are comin' to see Johnny die do you?"

John said, "No, didn't you know that the general store is havin' some kind of a contest today?"

"No, the only reason I was comin' was 'cause I promised Johnny I'd be there for 'im. What kind of contest?" Sam asked.

"I don't exactly know, but everybody who thinks they are rough and tough is gonna be there."

Sam turned to Bass and said, "Guess it's a good thing we brought you." He started to laugh as he slapped Bass on the back.

Bass just smiled and ducked his head, but his thoughts were on what kind of contest might be available for him. He always liked a good challenge, and if there was money involved, it could not be coming at a better time.

The streets were filled with people, and they seemed to be occupied with all kinds of trade and barter. It was eleven o'clock when the women and Sarah went to the sundry store after arranging for all of them to meet at the general store at one. The men all went to the big hill overlooking the town to witness the most unpleasant scheduled event.

A large crowd had gathered on the hilltop, and a good number were drinking and displaying conduct that was worrisome to the others. It looked as if there might be trouble from some of Johnny's drinking companions.

As if coming from some secret place, a group of Light Horsemen appeared in one swift move, each taking a spot next to one of those drinking. The captain of the Light Horse stood and said, "You fellows know that it is illegal for Indians to drink, and I am givin' you one second to pour out your liquor. If you hesitate, we'll arrest you and take you to the lockup. By rights,

I can lock you up now, but due to the day I'll forget it if you do as I say."

When the drinkers looked around, there was a Light Horseman standing within striking distance of each and every one of them. All but one immediately turned their bottle over and watched as the contents flowed to the ground.

The one that did not simply swayed a little and started to protest. Two policemen grabbed him by each arm, lifted him from the ground, pulled him backward and tied his hands behind him. Then they threw him into the back of a waiting wagon.

The captain then spoke, "In honor of Johnny, let's all try to act like the man he is."

About that time, Johnny walked toward Sam, grasped his hand and said, "I'm glad you are here, my friend and brother. It makes the day better. I've told the captain to give you my horse and other things. Get the best you can for 'em and see that my children get it." A tear came to his eyes, and he said softly, "Tell 'em I love 'em, and that I'm so sorry for the hardship I've caused 'em."

Minutes later, Johnny was led into the opening wearing full Cherokee dress. He was given a brightly colored blanket that he spread on the ground. He sat on the blanket, then looked to the heavens and began singing the haunting Cherokee death song. When he had finished, two officers took his outstretched arms and laid him on his back. Each placed one foot under his arm and the other against the side of his face, holding him motionless.

In a matter of fact manner, another officer quickly stepped forward from the crowd, placed his rifle on Johnny's heart and pulled the trigger. The blast was muzzled due to the closeness of the weapon, but Johnny's body recoiled upward from the impact.

The muzzle had been so close that the flame set Johnny's vest ablaze. The officer on his left removed his hat and snuffed out the fire, as if the event was an everyday occurrence. Another officer stepped forward and kneeled at Johnny's head, felt of his pulse and looked at his eyes and shut them before announcing, "It is done."

The crowd stood in silence for a moment. Then, one by one, they slowly started to move away. Sam and a few others walked to the dead man and stared at him in reverence for a moment, then turned to join those leaving.

Chapter 5

The Challenge

When Sam, Bass and John Ross reached the main part of town, they went first to the Captain's office to claim Johnny's belongings. These consisted of his pistol and a single-shot rifle. The entire lot was probably worth less than fifty dollars. However, when they went to claim his horse and saddle, Bass cast a knowing eye on the animal and said, "You know, I think this horse might be a runner."

"You think?"

"Well, I kinda like his looks. He seems sound, and look at his rump, lots of muscle there. His neck is long and his nostrils is wide open. Course you never know till you put 'im to the test, but at least he looks the part."

They took the horse and saddle to the center of town and followed the crowd to the general store. Posted on the wall were the rules of the upcoming contest. Sam read them out loud so Bass could know what was taking place.

"One says the entry fee is ten dollars. Two says that for the first part of the contest, all riders will race around the flag that is planted in the ground on the other side of Summit Ridge and back. If you fail to circle the flag, you are disqualified. The first ten riders will get their entry fee back and be allowed to go on with the contest. Each of the first ten will then have a shootin' contest. The ones that break four of six bottles with their pistols, shootin' from their hips at ten paces, will go to round three. Number three says that each remaining shooter, from a standin' position, will have three shots at a triangle at one hundred yards, with their rifle. The closest to the exact lower point on the triangle will be the winner. The winner gets one hundred dollars guaranteed, plus whatever money is left from the remaining entry fees."

Sam turned to Bass and said, "You gonna do that?"

"Sure, ain't you? If'n that horse of Johnny's is what I think, he sure could win your entry fee back, and if'n he did that, he'd bring more money for Johnny's kids."

"Well, that's a thought. Do you think he could?" Sam asked.

"Here's ten dollars. Go enter me in the contest. While you're doin' that, I'll go breeze 'im and come back and tell you. Say, how far is that there Summit Ridge?"

Sam stopped and thought, "I'd guess it's 'bout a mile."

"So the race is more than two miles."

"Yeah, I'd guess."

Bass said, "That's all I needs to know."

***

When Bass returned, he said, "That feller has a lot of heart. Course it depends on what he's up against. I'll tell you what I'll do. I'll give you five of the ten dollars so if he loses, we ain't busted ourselves, and if he comes in the first ten, he makes the kids more money. Is that a deal?"

Sam smiled and said, "Deal."

As the contestants gathered for the start of the race, Sam turned to Bass and said, "Great day in the mornin', I think I'm in way over my head. There must be over a hundred here."

Bass, with a big grin, said, "Just means there is more money in the pot. Don't worry if that horse can give you a run. I'll help all I can."

Mr. Tilley, the owner of the general store, rode a horse to the front of the gathering before saying, "Now, remember, you have to circle the flag on this leg or you're disqualified. I got lookouts on the flag. Go when I fire my pistol."

He then rode about two hundred yards in front of the humongous gathering of men before turning to face them. He raised his pistol and held it there. Time seemed to stand still, but at last a puff of smoke left his gun, followed by the roar.

Mayhem broke out with all of the horses jockeying for position. Bass, however, stayed back and let the eager take the beating. He had advised Sam that his horse should fight for the lead and hope he had the heart for the finish. Bass knew that King could finish and there was no need to possibly get bumped in the fracas.

As the race began to take its toll, some riders who had consumed too much liquor waiting for the race, started falling from their saddles. Some horses clipped the heels of those they were following and fell with their riders. Many of the riders were bumping their horses side to side, causing the horses to lose stride and valuable energy.

When Bass and King topped Summit Ridge, there were about twenty horses in front of them, and Sam was one of those. Bass smiled at the progress as he leaned next to King's ear and said, "Now is the time, boy. You need to show 'em who's the real King."

Bass could feel King's strides get longer and the frequency greater. By the time the pair circled the flag, there were only about fifteen horses in front of them. Sam's mount was holding his own.

Bass pushed King one more time, and his great heart answered the call. As they topped Summit Ridge, on the way back toward town, there were only twelve riders in front. Bass pushed King up behind Sam's horse and held him there. He shouted to Sam, "Give 'im the whip! You gotta make your move!"

Sam did as he was told and shortly was up to tenth place with Bass still right behind him. They were quickly gaining on two horses that were showing signs of weakness. Things were looking good for both Sam and Bass when suddenly the thunder of hoofs could be heard approaching from the rear.

As this strange horse approached, Sam and Bass passed the two struggling horses and now were in ninth and tenth place.

Bass kept King to the rear of Sam and again shouted, "It's only about two hundred yards to the finish. You gotta lay down on 'im."

Sam's horse showed that he still had life, and Bass knew that he had to get it out of him. Bass took a long look out of the corner of his eye and saw the horse behind them was bearing down on them from the left.

Bass timed it to the best of his ability. When he thought the horse was just to his left, he slowly pulled King to the left, causing the approaching horse to veer left with him. Sam's horse then got several yards in front.

After King had caused the other horse to lose stride, Bass gave King his head and quickly caught up to Sam. They both crossed the finish line in a ninth and tenth place tie.

When the last group of riders at last came to a stop, it was mayhem. Some struggled, while others walked in, and, on a few occasions, the riders came walking in leading their horses. It had been an all-out race, and the ten winners were quickly hurried to a position on the edge of town where the contest field had been prepared.

Bass and Sam both gave their horses to Little Sam, instructing him to walk and bathe the horses first, then carefully give them water and feed. The two men then strapped on their weapons and walked to the field.

Of course, they were followed by a throng of people, all anticipating a very exciting show.

Mr. Tilley was no fool. He had beer wagons stationed nearby, and food vendors were working the crowd like this might be everyone's last meal.

The men took their time stepping to the line, for the purpose of drawing to see the sequence in which they would shoot. The race had been much harder on them than they had expected. It was a proven fact that these men were tough or they would not have made it this far. The real difference was that now strength did not play nearly as great a role in the outcome of the contest. Skill, alone, was going to determine the winner.

As the ten qualifiers started to approach the firing line, a well-dressed man with riding boots and pants rushed from the crowd and said in an English accent, "Wait just a bloody moment here. This black bastard cheated me out of a place. He intentionally pulled his horse in front of mine, and I demand satisfaction!"

He had an ivory-handled pistol in his holster, facing with the handle to the right and at a forty-five degree angle, resting nearly in the center of his left leg.

Bass turned toward him. Bass' eyes narrowed as he apprised this man who obviously was from some place that Bass had never known.

Mr. Tilley rushed in and immediately tried to get control of the situation.

"Mister, my observers say that your horse didn't pass the flag. Accordin' to the well-explained rules, it makes no difference where you placed. You are disqualified. Now please stand back and let the real qualifiers continue with the contest."

"My name is English Bob, and I would bloody well appreciate it if you would address me properly."

Bass could see the tall Englishman was still fuming, so he decided that he might as well continue with the goading.

"Sir, it is beyond me why you cheated. The mare you were on was a fine mount, and she could've finished in the top ten if she'd been handled properly."

English Bob's face started to turn red and his eyes narrowed, as if trying to burn a hole through Bass.

"She certainly is a great mare. I brought her from my father's stable in England, and she was the best of the lot. If she had not been so stubborn and had made the turn at the flag, none of this would have happened."

Bass continued, "To make this fair, here is what I'm willin' to do. You seem to believe that you would win the shootin' contest. So, if Mr. Tilley will allow it, I'm willin' to make you a challenge. You truly must be one of the most feared persons to ever grace Indian Territory, so if you need a chance to prove yourself, I'll challenge you to a shoot out. We'll use the same rules that were already in place, just the two of us, except the first one to miss the target looses. The wager is simple. If I lose, I will give you my spot in the official shootout. There must be at least eight hundred in the pot. I'll also give you my horse. Now, if you lose, you'll give me four hundred dollars and your mare. Fair enough?"

The crowd was now nearly silent. They had never heard such a wager, and they seemed to be taking turns breathing. They wanted to hear and remember every word that was spoken between these two totally different men.

The Englishman looked long and hard at Bass. He was not accustomed to an underling even speaking to him, much less laying out rules and regulations. He was fuming inside, and it was so strong that it showed in not only his face, but in the way he stood and the way he carried himself. It appeared as though he wanted to strike Bass across the face, as he had so often done in his home country when a servant had dared to even speak to him.

Instead, English Bob shouted, "Done!"

Bass said, "Now give Mr. Tilley the four hundred dollars to hold until after the match. You have four hundred dollars, don't you?"

"I am good for it on my word as an Englishman."

"In England, you might be a gentleman, but this is Indian Territory, and no one's good here for four hundred dollars. So, if'n you got it, go get it, and if'n you don't have it, then stop runnin' your funny soundin' mouth."

English Bob turned and leaped from the platform, pushed his way through the crowd and stomped toward the hotel.

The moment he was gone, the crowd became alive. People began pushing and shoving, grabbing each other's arms. Pieces of paper were being passed and signed. Total chaos broke loose.

Mr. Tilley, who never missed a chance to make a buck, quickly hoisted a black board and started to write as rapidly as he could. Apparently, at some time in his shaded past, he had worked at a horse track. Now he was giving odds and had two men passing papers and receiving money in a frenzy.

Wagers were being made everywhere, people betting a quarter to tens of dollars with out of control excitement. Originally, Mr. Tilley planned to make a few extra dollars over the weekend. Now, he had a full-scale gambling operation.

Every man in town seemed caught up in the madness. People from parts unknown seemed to appear from thin air. The crowd swelled to at least a thousand, more than the town's total population.

About this time, Mr. Tilley saw English Bob leave the hotel. The storekeeper placed his face close to Bass' ear and said, "If you beat 'im, I'll give you an extra two hundred dollars. The confederates here have gone crazy thinkin' that a darkey surely can't defeat an Englishman in any kind of a contest. I've a lot ridin' on you, and I need to make sure you win."

Bass turned and smiled. "Mr. Tilley, I'll take your money, but I've a lot ridin' on this wager, and I aim to collect it. Don't worry."

While they were talking, Bass was cleaning his pistol. He wanted nothing to stand in his way of putting this uppity foreigner in his place. In fact, he began to think of this as one more step toward proving that he was as good as any man. He seemed to enjoy the fact that he had an opportunity to do it in front of a crowd.

English Bob pushed his way through the crowd. He was not acting like the gentleman he had purported to be. He was snarling at people, even thrusting aside the hand of those trying to wish him well.

Arriving in front of Mr. Tilley, English Bob withdrew a bag from his pocket and slapped it into Mr. Tilley's hand. Mr. Tilley winced with the impact, but quickly opened it and assured Bass that the money was there.

Bass nodded, and then confidently said, "Let's get started. Now, Bob, you need to calm down a little. You don't want to give me too great an advantage."

English Bob's face again turned red, and he said with only slightly restrained anger, "My name is English Bob."

"Oh, excuse me," Bass said, a smile crossing his face. "I nearly forgot your first name."

Mr. Tilley had twelve bottles placed on a bench ten yards from the starting line.

He then said, "All of you people listen. I want no disputes after this is over. Each shooter will fire three rounds at a time. He must draw his pistol on each round and cannot raise his pistol higher than his second button from the bottom. If he does, then it is counted as a miss. The first person to miss two bottles is disqualified, and the total wager goes to the winner. You all got that? English Bob, as the challenged, you have your choice whether to go first or second."

English Bob got in a verbal jab. "I will go first just to show this low life what a real man is like."

He stepped to the line and in quick succession fired the three rounds. All of the bottles vanished from the bench.

Bass followed, duplicating the feat.

The two men repeated their shooting skills again and again until both had fired twelve round each, without a miss.

Mr. Tilley called the two men together for a private discussion. He then stepped in front of the very impressed crowd and said, "We are movin' the bench back to twenty paces. All the other rules are the same."

The Englishman shot first and left one bottle standing. Bass followed, breaking all of his bottles.

The Englishman shot again, this time breaking all of his targets. Bass followed, leaving one bottle standing. The match was now a tie. The next man to miss would lose the wager.

The Englishman fired his rounds again. He missed the last bottle.

Bass took the line. This time, he seemed to crouch a little lower. He drew and fired. The first bottle shattered. He repeated the shot, sending the second bottle into the air.

While there were at least a thousand people watching, there was total silence.

A miss would tie the two men. A hit and Bass would be the winner.

Bass took a deep breath and remembered all the things he had told Little Sam. He pulled his pistol and fired. The bottle seemed to be caught in suspension. It finally spun around as if it was a man, fell from the bench and shattered on the ground.

The crowd went wild, some cheering and shouting while others were cursing and swearing. People started running back and forth to find those that owed money and a mad rush was made toward Mr. Tilley. He held up his hands and said, "Calm, calm. I will redeem all of the wagers at the store when you present your slips. Right now, we have to finish the original contest."

A crowd gathered around Bass, shaking his hand and patting him on the back. At the same moment, English Bob was kicking the ground with his knee-high riding boots and cussing so rapidly that few could understand what language he was speaking.

Sam worked his way to Bass and with a huge smile hugged his neck. While they were in the embrace, Bass said, "Find John quickly, tell 'im to go get the Englishman's horse and put it with ours at the livery stable. He should get in the loft with the shotgun. I don't trust this man, and I can just see 'im takin' the horse and runnin' for it."

For good measure, Bass added, "You and I have a contest to finish here, so do it fast."

Of the ten qualifiers, only four hit at least four bottles. As they were walking toward the rifle range, Sam grabbed Bass and pulled him toward the other Indian that had qualified.

"Bass I want you to meet an old friend of mine. This is Sam Sixkiller."

Bass stopped in his tracks. He narrowed his eyes as he stuck out his huge hand. "Are all you Cherokees killers?"

Sam Sixkiller said, "No some of us are lovers, but we don't like to be called that. But I can't wait 'til you meet Joseph Tenkiller."

They all broke out in laughter and slapped each other on the back, the small joke was a welcomed relief, especially for Bass. He had put King at risk, and while he had the confidence that he would win, the sheer thought that he might lose his prized possession had placed an extra burden on him.

The rifle range was no challenge for Bass, and the only time that there was any doubt as to whom the winner might be was when Sam Sixkiller tied him on the last shot. The shoot-off only lasted one more round, when Bass placed his shot squarely in the point of the triangle.

Chapter 6

The Trip Home

At the conclusion of the contest, Bass and Sam rushed to the livery stable to make sure all was well. It was extremely important that John be relieved or maybe even backed up in his efforts to secure the new mare. Bass and Sam both had an uneasy feeling about the Englishman and felt they were asking too much for John to take on this dangerous responsibility by himself.

They were relieved, upon arrival, that all was quiet and in order. This gave Bass time to evaluate his new addition. She was sound and showed the quality that he had hoped. He was already thinking about the great offspring from the mating of King and the new mare.

Bass now needed to go to the general store to collect the rest of his earnings. He did not know exactly how much it would be, but knew that it could possibly be the economic boost that he and Jane needed to really put their lives in financial security. Before leaving to collect, however, he asked Sam and John to take the horse to the campsite where Bass would meet them and their families for the return home.

Bass' journey to the store was slowed by well-wishers, people who offered him congratulations, slaps on the back and hearty handshakes. He could not help but notice that several people were equally standoffish and appeared to not only be upset, but showing signs of hostility.

These reactions did not bother him that much. He knew that losers often can't deal with their defeats, and hopefully they learned from their mistakes.

When he got to the store, Mr. Tilley was busy paying out the funds he had lost in the wagers, but his face showed that the losses were just a formality. He had gained much more on the winning side, and his store sales had more than doubled with the increased flow of people the event had drawn to town.

When Mr. Tilley got a break, he motioned for Bass to come to the back room.

Mr. Tilley easily turned and started in that direction, but Bass had to struggle through the people who wanted to shake his hand and just be close to him. Bass was as cordial as he could be, but he also was eager to reach the back room to collect his earnings.

Mr. Tilley waited at the door until Bass arrived. He then slipped his key in the lock, opened the door and the two men entered. There, on the desk, was a pile of money like Bass had never seen. Coins and bills were scattered from one side of the desk to the other. Most of the coins were in stacks, and the bills were placed in stacks by denominations.

Tilley motioned for Bass to take a seat opposite his desk. First clearing his throat, he then said, "Bass you did right nicely today. I've figured it up, and the total comin' from the entry fees is eight hundred and sixty dollars, plus one hundred dollars for the win and the two hundred that I said I'd add. That comes to eleven hundred and sixty dollars, a right promisin' sum of money."

Bass sat for a moment, then said, "I think you forgot the twenty dollars you owe Sam and me for comin' in the top ten, and the four hundred dollars you were holdin' from the Englishman."

"Oh, I did, didn't I?" Mr. Tilley smoothly said, applying pencil to paper as he refigured. "Well, that makes it fifteen hundred and eighty dollars. What in the world are you gonna do with it?"

"I got plans. The first is to go to Texas and see if I can get my mama out of there, and the second one is probably to buy me some land and start my own farm and horse operation. Probably the most immediate thing is for me to get married."

"Get married! Now that is a soberin' thought."

"Yep, sure is. But I have this young lady that has turned out to be just perfect for me, and I'd just like to settle down and become the ordinary man I should be."

"Sounds like this day's really been the start of a new beginnin' for you, I wish you well."

Mr. Tilley counted out the money, an impressive stack. He placed it in a sack and pushed it across the desk.

"Now be careful with that. You know it will be mighty tempting to a lot of people."

Bass pulled one of his pistols out and checked it. "I think that it should be safe with me until I can get it to the bank."

"I am sure it will," Mr. Tilley said.

***

Bass made the trip to the bank, where he was greeted with open arms.

It was unusual for a black man to be welcomed in the bank, but the bankers knew he was bringing money and that certainly altered their attitude.

After leaving the bank, Bass returned to the campsite where he was warmly welcomed by Jane and the others. They had brought the mare and the other horses to the camp, and all were relaxing after an exciting and extremely profitable day.

Bass did notice that Johnny's horse was not amongst the tie out. He asked Sam about it.

"You were exactly right. His bein' in the top ten greatly increased his value, and I was able to sell 'im for two hundred dollars. This is money that I know will be of great help to Johnny's kids, and I thank you for makin' the suggestion. Of course, the help you gave him didn't hurt."

"Sam here is the five dollars you put up for the entry, and I have something here that we'll enjoy."

Bass pulled a smoked ham out of a sack, and the entire group let out a cry of excitement.

"Ain't it funny what some money can do to change your life? We'll eat like we're somebody tonight."

The visit lasted into the night, and it was filled with laughter and great friendship. Little Sam and Sarah played with the Ross children, but from time to time, Little Sam would come to sit next to Bass. It was obvious that he held this man in great admiration, and just being close was satisfying to the young boy.

Due to the possibility of people wanting to steal what they had gained in the day, the three men took turns keeping watch, but the night passed peacefully.

After breakfast, the wagon was loaded, and the group started for home.

The day was warm, and the recent rains had worked its wonders. The buds on the trees were exploding, and the grass seemed as though you could actually see it grow. What a beautiful greeting for people who were on the verge of having a tumultuous change in their lives.

The mare was tied to the back of the wagon, and Bass, Sam, John and Little Sam were trailing behind. From time to time, Bass would ride up to the side of the wagon just to stare and smile at Jane. His smiles were returned, and the feelings the two shared were obvious to all.

About three miles from town, however, the tranquility quickly ended. First, there was a rifle crack that sent a projectile directly across Bass' vest, so close that it took a button off as it passed. John, who was on Bass' right, was not as lucky. The bullet penetrated his shoulder, and he nearly fell from his horse.

Sam grabbed John, steadying him in his saddle. Bass pulled his pistol and turned his horse toward the trees from where the shot had come. He shouted to Little Sam to ride to the wagon and get them moving ahead.

"Get to some place and take cover. Sam, take John and join them. I'll take the rear and hold 'em off," shouted Bass.

As the others quickly moved ahead, Bass slowed King as he continued moving toward the escaping wagon, but kept his eyes on the trees. His wait was short when another rifle shot rang out, followed by movement among the trees of at least ten riders.

Bass fired at them, but the distance was too great, and he knew it. Nonetheless, his shots sent a warning to the attackers letting them know they were in for a fight.

He turned, gave King his head and followed in the direction of the wagon.

As he approached an outcropping of rocks, he heard a rifle fire on his right. He focused on the smoke and saw that Sam had abandoned the wagon and taken cover in the rocks. He was covering Bass' back. Bass turned King into the rocks, pulled his Spencer from the boot and rushed to join Sam.

Sam and Bass both took aim and fired into the oncoming riders. Their shots were on the mark with two riders falling from their saddles. Sam and Bass both fired again, and one more attacker fell to the dust.

Bass said, "We can't let them get past us, so make your shots count."

The next volley took two more riders to the ground. That's when the attackers realized they could not afford to continue their assault head-on. They quickly veered to the left and dismounted into the rocks. In an instant, the rocks were ablaze with rifle fire.

Now a pitched battle was clearly under way. The bullets were whizzing over the heads of Bass and Sam, glancing off the rocks that were giving the two men much needed cover. The firing was so intense that it was very difficult for the pair to take the time to get a clean shot. They had to be satisfied that they were able to keep the aggressors at bay.

This futile position was assisting the escape of the wagon, but showed no promise for a solution to the immediate circumstance.

Bass surveyed the terrain before turning to Sam. "If you can keep 'em busy, I think I can go up this ridge and get to a position to shoot down on 'em."

Sam said, "I got plenty of ammunition, and if you think you can get us some relief, go to it."

Bass immediately started up the ridge, moving as quickly as possible. He worked his way among the boulders and trees toward the position that he knew would mean a total change of advantage for them. The climb was steeper than he had thought; forcing him to lay down the Spencer so he could use both hands to pull himself up the steep bank. The discarding of the rifle also enabled him to move much faster.

As he was pulling himself up, he looked up to see a renegade coming down the trail toward him. Unfortunately for Bass, both of his hands were full of rocks and small trees to assist him in his climb. The assailant was standing on solid ground, which gave him a tremendous advantage. As Bass struggled to the top of the crest, the attacker rapidly raised his rifle and fired.

Bass gave one great pull and now was on his stomach, but still at the mercy of his opponent. In his haste, the man's attempt to shoot Bass had miraculously missed his target. The man instantly dropped his rifle and went for his pistol. This brief move gave Bass time to roll to his side where he rapidly drew his pistol. Bass fired before his adversary could even clear his holster, hitting him squarely in the center of his chest. To ensure his safety, he fired again as the man fell to the ground.

Bass continued his roll and quickly scrambled to his feet. He rushed to a point where he was sure he had the position on the attackers, only to be greeted by an unwanted sight.

The attackers must have figured that Sam was alone, so they mounted their horses and ridden directly toward him. Sam was able to drop one of the riders, but by the time he had prepared to fire again, the remaining riders breezed past him. He fired at them in their flight, but in such hurriedness, his effort missed its mark.

As Bass watched the men ride off, he noticed that while the riders looked like regular cowboys, one of them had on highly polished knee-high riding boots.

Bass started running as fast as he could to get back down the ridge and to his horse, but the distance was great and the climb was slow. By the time he reached King, Sam had already mounted and was giving pursuit. Bass grabbed his rifle and vaulted into the saddle.

Bass knew that the wagon had a considerable head start, but the race was on. He hoped they had reached the cover of Ross' neighbor's house. Bass felt confident that if they had, they would be able to stand off the pursuers until Sam could get there.

As he moved at full speed, he listened for gunshots, but never heard any. He concluded that, at least for the moment, all was well. As he rounded a bend, he was shocked to see Little Sam riding at full speed directly toward him.

Little Sam held up his hand and pulled his pony to a halt.

Bass did not understand, but pulled King to a halt beside him.

Bass shouted. "What has happened?"

Little Sam could not look Bass in the eyes. The boy kept his head down while searching for words. His discomfort was evident. Finally, he spoke. "Mr. Bass, it's not good." Tears started to run down his face. "Mr. Bass, the wagon wrecked, and people are hurt."

"Who is hurt, and how bad?" Bass demanded, getting an uneasy feeling.

"Well, most everybody is hurt, but, but..."

Now tears were starting to stream from the boy's eyes.

"What, what?" Bass asked.

"Miss Jane, Miss Jane is dead," Little Sam stammered.

Bass was frozen in the moment. In seconds, he quickly turned King and rode full speed down the road.

When he got to the wagon, there were people strewn all around the wreckage. Sam was moving from one to the other, trying to make them as comfortable as possible.

Lying next to a large rock was someone with a blanket covering the face, but the dress and shoes left no doubt as to who was under it.

Bass dismounted and rushed to the blanket-covered body. He stopped, then pulled the covering back slowly. There was the face of the woman who had made him so happy, the woman he had planned to make his wife. Now she and all their plans were before him, lifeless.

Bass knelt beside her for several minutes. Tears came to his eyes. He felt that a hole had replaced his insides. He had trouble getting his breath. He held her lifeless hand, and then gently touched it to his face. He stroked her cheek, hoping for some sign of movement, but the life was gone. He knew it, all the while not wanting to acknowledge the obvious.

Finally, he gained control, stood and asked of anyone there to answer, "What happened here?" His deep voice had a sternness that no one had ever heard.

Little Sam walked toward him, placed his arms around his waist and let out a choked sob. The boy slowly released his grip and stepped back. "I was trying to stay with the wagon when it just hit a rock and went in the air. Everyone was thrown out, and Miss Jane's head hit that rock. She never moved after that."

"Then what happened?" Bass asked.

"Those men came and searched through the stuff in the wagon. They untied the mare and high-tailed it as soon as they saw Papa coming."

"Did you know any of 'em?" Bass continued exhibiting a deadly focus.

"No. There were four of 'em, but one of 'em had on high boots. And another was wearin' his pistol on his left hip. Mr. Bass, I woulda fought 'em, but I had no gun. I'm so sorry I couldn't save Miss Jane. I'm so sorry," Little Sam said with more sorrow and regret than any young boy should ever feel.

Bass stood and stared into space. He finally looked down at Little Sam and said, "I know you woulda done what you coulda, but don't ever worry that I would question your bravery. I need you now to help take care of your family. I got to go and finish some business."

He turned to see the others and was pleased that at least the others he loved so much were not in bad shape. Sarah limped toward him with huge tears running down her cheeks. She reached up for him to pick her up.

He instantly followed the move and pulled her close to him. She hugged his neck and placed kisses on his cheek. Her tears were so great that she soon made the collar of his shirt wet.

"Sam, can you take care of all this?" Bass asked. "I've got somethin' to do. I need you to keep everyone as comfortable as you can while I send you a wagon and a doctor. I'll not be back for a spell. I've got a load of hell that needs deliverin'."

Chapter 7

English Bob

Bass turned and ran to King. He mounted and turned toward town, then pulled up and looked one more time at the blanket-covered body before asking Little Sam, "They did head back to town, didn't they?"

"I'm not sure. They went toward those trees. The mare was limping from the crash, but I think I could hear them turning back toward town."

"Well, I'll trail 'em to make sure."

He turned for the trees. As soon as he left the meadow, he was riding with his head down, looking for tracks. Luckily, the rain that had fallen the past days made the trail open and clear. With this advantage, Bass was able to pick up his pace, feeling certain he would soon overtake them, especially if they were leading the lame mare. After some distance, the trail broke out into a meadow where Bass put King in full stride. As the trail neared the trees, he noticed that three riders went toward town, while the rider leading the mare turned to the right and started heading south.

He brought King to a halt, and then sat for a moment. He knew that the one with the mare was English Bob, who must have really cared for the horse. That meant the English man would stop in a while to check on her condition, and that if she were hurt, he probably would stop and let her heal. After all, if he would go to this much trouble to get her back, he surely would not force her to run injured and stand the chance of ruining or even killing her.

Bass did not know who the others were, but he had no intention of allowing them to escape the justice he envisioned. Now satisfied that they were heading back to town, Bass reasoned that with the crowd still there, the men could easily blend in, making it impossible to locate them.

With that thought, he turned King toward town and put him in full stride. Hopefully, he could catch them before they got entwined in the crowd.

As he surmised, the town was still full of people doing their shopping. Bass immediately began looking for any horses that looked as if they just had arrived, having been ridden hard. Slowly walking King down the street, Bass eyed each animal.

In the second block, he saw Sam Sixkiller coming toward him.

As the two men neared each other, Bass quickly said, "Sam, I need your help. Have you seen three riders just come into town with spent horses?"

"Why?"

"They just killed my girl and shot John Ross."

Sam appeared shocked. "What happened?" he asked.

"I don't have time to explain, but if you'd get the doc and send a wagon towards the Ross place, I'd appreciate it. There're a lot of people who need help. There're also a lot of bodies, so you'd better take some of the Light Horse with you," Bass said, suddenly eager to continue his search.

"I'll send the people, but I'm staying with you to help," Sam said. "You go on down the street toward the livery, and as soon as I can, I'll catch up with you. They're probably at the saloon. If not, then they're probably at the livery. So, if I don't hear a ruckus, I'll meet you in front of the saloon."

"Good," Bass said, turning to tie King to a rail. He then stepped into the shade of the overhang, pulled his Remington and reloaded.

The shade worked for him, and he used it to his advantage as he approached the livery stable. He rushed from the shadow to the side of the barn where he stopped and listened. Not hearing any voices, he entered the door with his pistols in his hands.

Clarence, the owner, dropped his pail of water and shouted, "Don't shoot! For god's sake, don't shoot!" His eyes were wide, and he was as pale as buttermilk. He stood frozen, carefully raising his hands.

Bass asked, "There been three fellers in here in the last few minutes?"

"No, but three guys just left their horses tied out back by the water trough. Then they went back toward the saloon."

"That's all I wanted to know."

Bass went to the back door and looked at the horses. They surely were well used, and he thought he recognized one of them.

Bass began slowly walking down the boardwalk toward the saloon. As he passed, several people attempted to shake his hand to congratulate him for his victory in the shoot off, but the intense expression on his face and the fire in his eyes quickly changed their minds. He paused at the side of a building and waited for Sixkiller. When Sam arrived, Bass said, "Is the saloon full of people?"

"It's packed."

"You go to the back door. I don't aim for these bastards to get away.

One of 'em is left-handed, and one's got on a red shirt. I think they will show themselves when I enter, but I don't know.

"If they go out the back," Bass continued, "Stop 'em any way you can. They got a price to pay, and today is collection day."

Sam assured Bass, "Don't worry. I've already sent two Light Horse back there with shotguns. There's no way they're leavin'."

"I thank you. Go now. I'll give you time to get set, and then I'm goin' in," Bass said.

While Bass waited, several men started to enter the saloon, but when they saw him standing by the door looking even bigger than usual, with the determination on his face that left no doubt he was full of hostility, their thirst rapidly faded. They turned and speedily retreated.

Bass pulled down his broad-brimmed hat; made sure his pistols were loose in their holsters and entered. He stepped three or four feet inside the darkened room, making sure that the light behind the door outlined him.

He had every intention of being noticed; truly desiring that those he pursued would know he was there. In his state of mind, he took none of his usual precautions. He simply hoped the men he sought would make a play and save him the trouble of having to locate them in the crowd.

Slowly, the voices and laughter in the saloon faded, giving way to absolute silence in the big room. The silence was broken only by mummers as heads turned toward the door.

As his eyes adjusted to the dimness of the room, his head turned from side to side, sizing up the occupants. Unable to locate his prey, he announced in a low but firm voice, "I'm lookin' for three bastards that just got here. If you're standin' next to 'em, I'd advise you to get clear."

His proclamation brought an unexpected reaction.

Chairs scooted across the floor with several men jumping to their feet, and rushed for the door, totally blocking Bass' view as they ran by and in front of him. As the last few frightened men passed him, a shot rang out followed by several more. These reports started to fill the room with smoke, but the flashes pinpointed the location of his target.

When the shots first sounded, Bass pulled his pistols and fell to the right to reduce his silhouette. He stumbled over a man who had been hit by the volley and then fell to the floor. Bass struggled to untangle himself from the man and the chairs. By the time he had regained his balance, all he could see was the outline of three men running out the back door.

Bass heard the shout of, "Halt and drop 'em!"

The orders were immediately followed by the sound of several pistol shots, followed by the roar of numerous shotgun blasts.

Bass pushed through the tables and chairs, which were now strewn about the room. He rushed to the back door, reaching it in time to see a halo of smoke hanging over three bodies lying in different states of bloody disarray.

Sixkiller stepped from behind the corner of the outhouse and said, "Bass, I told you they'd not get away. We wanted to hold 'em for court, but they made the choice."

Bass stood silently for a moment, staring at the bodies. He saw what was left of the red shirt. It was hard to tell whether it was the original color or whether the blood gave it that hue. He observed the left-handed holster on another, and then concluded that the third body identified himself by his presence alone.

Bass took a deep breath, then turned toward Sixkiller and said, "Sam looks like you and the boys took care of three of my problems. I still have English Bob to go after."

"English Bob? Is he behind this?" Sam asked.

"Seems like he thought he wanted his mare back — and the money that I won and took from 'im."

Bass paused for a moment before adding, "I'd of give it all to 'im if I'd known what it'd cost."

"Do you know where he went?"

"No, but he is leading the mare, and she is lame. He can't move too fast, if he moves at all. I got to go and get Jane and check on the Mankillers. A Englishman with a lame mare won't be hard to trail."

Chapter 8

The Pursuit

The big sorrel mare was going to be the Englishman's undoing. Bass knew that he could catch up to him in due time, so for now, he had important things that needed his attention. He had to get back to Jane and see if there was anything else that the Mankillers needed before he made the painful trek back to the Upton's to deliver their daughter.

As he thought about it, the trip seemed to be more painful than he first considered. This second trip would mean that the only times he had visited Mrs. Upton was when it had to do with the death of a family member. While several months had passed since he last saw them, it still would be no easy task.

His trip back to the Mankiller homestead was filled with thoughts of Jane, how she had so completely changed his life. Her continual humor and liveliness, a source of happiness for him, that would be irreplaceable. Bass recalled Jane's love of the horses, how she had spent so many hours working to help him make his life dreams become more of a reality. His loss seemed too much.

Then, in consolation, he remembered the one thing that had always driven him; the idea that things happen when they happen because they are supposed to happen. Everything has its reasons, and time is the thing that brings those things to pass.

Bass finally arrived at the Mankillers', where he found the family in total disarray. The loss of Jane apparently was nearly as hard on them as it was on him. Bass had not realized how much she had become part of the family, and how she and Lidia had become like sisters. The children had become attached to her playfulness and good cheer. Plus, she had created a special bond by being able to help them with their schoolwork when Lidia was too occupied.

Sam greeted Bass as he dismounted. As they shook hands, Sam pulled Bass close, placing his arms around Bass' broad shoulders. He even placed his cheek against Bass' and said, "I'm sorry, so, so sorry. I don't know what else to say except that I'm with you in your heart, and I will support you in any way, my brother."

Bass responded after a few seconds. "At least I had her for a little while, and she did light life for all of us. I thank you for your words. It's greatly comfortin' at this time."

They stayed in the arms and grips of each other for some time. Then Bass said, "How are the children and Lidia?"

"They are just buggered up a little. Their real pain is for Jane. Little Sam says he wants to go with you after English Bob."

"He can do me a greater favor by stayin' here and takin' care of Blaze and the other horses. I figure the trail will be long and hard, and I don't need to be worrin' 'bout stuff back here."

Little Sam came out of the house and walked to the men. He paused for a moment, then wrapped his arms around Bass and said, "I really wanted to protect Jane and the others. I am sorry I failed."

"You did all you could, and I'm just glad that you were near. Now, I want you to do somethin' for me and Jane. Make sure the horses are well cared for, especially Blaze. You know how much she cared for him, and I kinda figure she left him for you to care for."

Little Sam said, "I'll do all I can to make Jane proud, if that's what you want, but I'd really like to go with you."

"I know you would," Bass said, looking with love at the boy. "Someday maybe we can ride together, but right at this time, you can be more help to me givin' good care to the horses. It'll take a heap of worry off'en my mind, and I just wanta have one thing on it, and that is gettin' Bob."

Turning to the boy's father, Bass said, "Sam spread the word. I'm taking Jane back to the Seminole village, and anyone who has seen English Bob should try to get word to me. After I finish this painful task, I aim to spend full time on bringin' 'im down."

Bass then went in the house to speak with Lidia and Sarah. When he told them of his plans, Lidia said nothing, but immediately began to prepare him food for the trail. She knew that once he had set his mind to something, the only thing she could do was support him.

Sarah ran to him and jumped into his arms. She had a huge knot on her head that surely was causing her pain, but she appeared to forget about it as she tried to comfort Bass.

She looked in Bass' eyes, and the tears rolled down her face. She wrapped her arms around his neck and pulled him close to her. When her cheek reached his, she let out a sigh and gripped him even tighter.

Bass left the Mankillers that evening. With Jane strapped to a pack-horse, he decided to keep on the road until he reached his destination. He remembered the trail well, for it had been a path to happiness that would never leave his mind.

After traveling all night, it was past midday when he arrived in the village. He was shocked that the people seemed to know that he was coming, but he was reminded that word travels fast in Indian country. It seems to travel on the wind.

The Upton family was waiting his arrival, a service already had been prepared. It took little time to lay Jane to rest. Afterwards, Mrs. Upton wanted to talk. It was a different type of conversation this time. Bass knew many things that needed to be shared with her and her son. The talk must have helped all involved. They had a mutual feeling that if good words helped Jane on her journey, then she was having a smooth trip.

The next morning, Bass rose early. He wanted to get a jump on the sun, but before he even got a saddle on King, a rider entered the village and found him.

"I hear you're lookin' for a foreigner with a sorrel mare," the man said in Seminole.

"Right."

"It is said that he is on the road south toward the Texas country. He should be somewhere north of Boggy Depot 'bout now. Ain't movin' too fast. The mare is gimpy, and he ain't pushin' her."

"Thanks. How far do you think he is from here?"

"If'n you hurry, you could probably catch 'im in half a day. But if you don't, I'd bet he stops at Curly Ann's place. You can get rubbed, tubbed, scrubbed and grubbed there, and if you ain't careful, they'll club you. But most men like the adventure."

"Where is this invitin' place?" Bass asked.

"It's 'bout five miles north of Boggy Creek, right on the trail."

"Thanks," Bass said. "I best be gettin' on. By the way, who are you, my friend?"

"I'm Jane's cousin, and I sure wish I could be there. I's figurin' that man needs a good killin', but I hears you is the man to do it. Good huntin' to you."

Bass put King in full gallop. He did not intend for English Bob to reach Curly Ann's. Knowing the Englishman, he might pay some low life to join him and make Bass' odds harder. There were too many bottom-feeding thugs just looking for easy money. This made the possibility of English Bob finding a band very likely.

Bass traveled smooth and steady. Even though he had a particular goal, he still studied the land and the markings. This was his first time in this part of Choctaw territory, and he didn't want to miss the opportunity to learn all he could in case he needed it in the future.

He had ridden hard for half a day. He felt he had surely covered enough ground to be near English Bob. However, he had seen no signs of him, so he was starting to wonder if he had been given correct information.

Bass slowed King, starting to observe more around him and listen closer. Soon, he reached the top of a crest; from here he could see a man walking in the meadow below. He rode King slowly down the ridge, making sure the man could see his approach.

As Bass neared, he raised his right hand and pulled King to a stop. He did not want the stranger to have any fear. The man, after stopping and assessing the stranger, continued toward him.

As he neared, Bass asked in Seminole, "Have you seen any one leading a blazed face sorrel mare, probably lame?"

The old Indian man looked long and hard at Bass, obviously trying to figure out a strange black man carrying two side arms, mounted on a huge horse and speaking Seminole.

Finally, the stranger spoke. "I saw a man like that a few hours ago, and the way he was travelin', I'd guess he was headed toward Curly Ann's place."

"Where is that?" Bass asked.

"'Bout a mile from here, over that hill and down in the valley by the creek. I thought every man knew where it was."

"I don't, but I guess it is time to learn. I want to thank you for your words. You need anything?"

"Jest a few more years," the man said with a shrug of his shoulders.

"Can't help you there, but can wish you the best," Bass responded.

"Same to you stranger. Say, ain't you that Reeves feller? I heard 'bout you in the past."

"Guess I am," Bass said. "By the way, do they serve Indians in there?"

"Mister, they'd serve the devil if he had the price."

Bass quickly formed a plan.

"Say, would you sell your blanket and hat?"

"Never really thought 'bout it," the Indian said. "Ain't much good, but it's all I got."

"Would you take twenty dollars for it?"

Bass had no more than gotten the words from his lips than the old man started shedding his garments.

"Where's the twenty?" he asked.

Bass reached in his pocket and handed him four five-dollar pieces.

The man took them with a smile, then said, "I heard you's a brave man, but you ain't too smart."

Bass just smiled, then turned King and ascended the hill. When he reached the top, he walked his stallion to the bottom, keeping his eyes alert for signs of the mare or anything else that would assure him he was closing in on his prey.

Bass decided to walk into the area through the trees that surrounded the large log building that sat next to a creek. The building had a large corral, and there were several horses inside. The first thing he wanted to do was check for the mare.

He approached the holding pen, easing up to the fence. He quickly spotted the mare. She looked fairly sound, but her right front leg had a bandage on it. Bass looked around, unable to resist the urge to crawl through the rails and inspect the mare. Up close, the bandage had the smell of turpentine, and it looked fresh.

Bass was relieved to see that at least the Englishman was trying to help the mare. He inspected the leg and felt that she was able to travel, but certainly not able to carry a load. The best thing for her would be time in a pasture where she could let nature take care of her problem.

Making sure that no one was watching, Bass led King into the corral and unsaddled him. He took off his big hat and vest. He carefully placed them in his saddlebag before taking his Spencer to a pile of hay. He hid it in the stack, making sure that the gun was totally concealed. The Spencer would draw too much attention to him, and his plan now was to avoid as much notice as possible.

Now, he placed the blanket around his shoulders, letting it fall around his thighs, pleased that it was just long enough to cover his pistols. He took the old man's hat and pulled it down as low as he could. It was a tight fit, but he felt it served its purpose.

Bass bent over a young sapling, using his knife to cut it down. He stripped the branches, and then cut the remaining stick into a six foot length. He removed all the bark where his hand might fit the new walking stick. Before he proceeded to the roadhouse, he checked his pistols and the extra cylinders in his belt.

Everything was just the way he wanted it. Bass stooped over and, using the walking stick in his left hand, slowly made his way toward the two-story log building. The front had two steps leading up to the porch, which extended the full length of the establishment. There were few windows in the building and only a single door leading from the porch inside. Since the weather was warm, the only thing covering the entrance was the latticed double swinging doors.

Bass played his role to the hilt. He had great difficulty climbing the stairs, and then grabbed his chest, as if he were having difficulty breathing. He stood on the porch in full view of those who might be looking his direction. He coughed several times and spit as much saliva as he could possibly muster, then again cleared his throat so that those inside could not help but notice him.

Bass leaned heavily on the stick, acting as if he were about to lose his balance. He slowly turned toward the door and limped to the entrance. He kept his head down while placing his right hand on top of the door. He slowly entered, dragging his leg a little, still leaning heavily on the stick. By peering just under the brim of the tattered hat, he was able to locate an empty chair and table against the back wall.

Bass moved toward the table, but he was constantly moving his eyes from side to side in an effort to locate English Bob. This search proved to be uneventful as he continued to the table.

He eased himself into the chair that faced the room, putting his back to the wall. He slumped over so that his face would be in the shadow of his hat brim.

He had not been seated long when a woman approached. "Hey, good lookin'. What'll you have?"

Bass kept his head down, but reached a shaking hand out from under the blanket and whispered, "Whiskey."

She said, "You got money?"

Bass slowly reached his hand into his pocket, pulled out a twenty-dollar gold piece and laid it on the table.

"Well, that's more like it. Maybe I could interest you in somethin' else later."

She turned and headed toward the bar.

As she was walking, Bass' eyes followed her, taking great care to notice every man she passed.

It became obvious that the Englishman was not in the room.

Bass chuckled to himself, "He must be gettin' rubbed or tubbed."

The upstairs had a walkway all the way around it with numerous doors along the hall. The only stairway was just to his right, making it very easy for him to completely observe those who were coming and going.

The woman returned with his drink and laid his change on the table. As she counted out the gold pieces, she pulled one back and said, "You know, for this 'en here, I could give you somethin' you ain't never had before."

Bass sat for a moment, and then said, "You got da whoopin' cough? I thinks I's had 'bout everythin' else. Thank you, but for now, I just needs a drink."

She laughed and placed the coin back on the table, before turning and walking away, still laughing.

Bass lifted the glass to his lips and took in about a quarter of the liquid. He held it in his mouth, just in case someone was watching. He then let it run back into the glass.

Time passed slowly. He would, from time to time pour some of the liquid on the floor later motioning for the woman to refill his glass. This went on for well over an hour. Bass was beginning to wonder if he had missed something.

He was just about to stand and work his way to the door, to make sure the mare was still in the corral, when he heard several horses approaching and sounds of laughter coming from the front.

He heard a man say, "Get down from there, and if you don't, you'll pay hell."

A woman's voice followed, "Keep your filthy hands off of me, you low-life son-of-a-bitch!"

This was followed by the sound of a hand slap and a shriek.

Shortly, the swinging doors opened, and a woman entered supported by a man on each arm. Her blonde hair was covering most of her face, but she showed signs of having been slapped. She was resisting, although clearly over matched.

One of the men grabbed her by the hair, pulled her face up and shouted to the room, "Is there anyone in here that would like to buy this bitch or maybe rent 'er for a spell?"

Bass looked up at the commotion and was stunned. Even after all this time, it was evident that the lady in distress was Miss Nancy, daughter of his former master. Bass looked twice to make sure. He had no doubt that this woman was the same person he had protected when he was a slave. This was the woman for whom he had spent a night in jail and faced lynching because he shot the man that tried to molest her.

The last time he had seen her was the night he was riding King at the Reeves Camp just before they had left for the first battle in Indian Territory. He recalled well seeing her jump into the buggy, hurrying away with that young man she was always visiting in Paris, when they went to the northeast Texas town to shop.

He remembered how upset Master Reeves was when she eloped and went to Indian Territory. Later, Bass heard that George, the boy she ran away with, had become somewhat successful as a storekeeper, and that Nancy seemed to be doing well.

Bass' first thought was to rise and force the men to let her go. Then he remembered that the reason he was here was to get revenge for the death of Jane.

What a strange position he found himself. Two of the four women with whom he had the most ties were now the center of his concerns, and at almost the same time.

Bass willed himself to sit still, telling himself that if he made a play, it would expose his hand and possibly let the Englishman escape.

While he sat, the two men continued to humiliate Miss Nancy. They were fondling and kissing her, all the while taking her from table to table and letting others do the same.

This action was working the crowd into frenzy. Bass finally decided that enough was enough. He had to make a move and hope that whatever happened with the Englishman, he would be able to deal with it when it was time.

Bass slowly stood and dropped the blanket from his shoulders. He took the tattered hat from his head and placed it on the table. Before he made a move toward the crowd that had now gathered around Miss Nancy, he took one more look at the doors above him. Noticing nothing different, he started to make his move.

In a low voice he asked, "How much do you want for 'er!" When there was no response, he spoke again, louder. "I said, how much do you want for 'er?" This time it was so loud that the walls of the room seemed to shake, causing the laughing to cease. The crowd slowly turned toward the source of the interruption of their fun. When they located Bass, they started to spread out, away from the center of their attention.

The two men who had brought in Nancy now looked at Bass. The first thing they noticed was his blackness, evidently not paying much attention to the two Remingtons hanging on his hips.

Still in a humorous mood, one of the men answered, "There ain't no nigger that can afford this fine piece of yellow-haired beauty."

Bass never flinched, "There ain't no white egg suckers that can live through the night touchin' that yellow-haired beauty."

The atmosphere suddenly changed from one of pleasure to one of all-out seriousness.

Bass said, "You boys have a choice to make. You can hand me the lady and ride out of here, or you can hope that someone knows your kin, so they can come and claim your stinkin', cold bodies."

The look on Bass' face showed that this was not a bluff. The bystanders started to move away from the three, who just moments earlier had been the center of entertainment.

The two men stared at Bass.

As Bass stood and observed them, he suddenly recognized them. "You boys' feet still sore?" he asked.

This took them by surprise, and they both began to look bewildered.

"I gave you one chance and hoped you'd change your ways. Looks like it failed. I had feared that I'd have to kill you one day. Looks like today's the day."

Now you could see the events sinking into the minds of the two men. They both started to recall the last time they had heard that voice, and they recalled the accuracy of his rifle shots. It was clear that they had no desire to relinquish the lady, but they had already tasted Bass' ire and wanted no more.

They pushed Miss Nancy toward Bass and immediately turned and ran for the door.

Bass caught her as she stumbled across the room and held her in his arms. She was sobbing and clutching his broad shoulders as if he were a life raft.

Bass never took his eyes off the other men in the room as he heard the horses leave the hitching post. He slowly backed away from them and pulled Nancy into the corner, seating her in a chair.

Without turning his back on the crowd, he leaned over and said, "Miss Nancy, relax. You're safe. I won't let nobody hurt you."

She placed her head on her arms folded on the table and began to cry. Bass put his huge hand on her head and repeated his promise for her not to worry.

Bass turned to the lady at the bar and said, "I want one of 'em rooms now."

The lady grabbed a key, rushed past him and started up the stairs. She now realized that the man she had mistaken for an old, simple drunk, was a man of force and determination.

Bass took Nancy by the arm and lifted her to her feet. He gently, but hurriedly, took her up the stairs to the room that the bar maid had opened. He placed her on the bed and said, "Now get some rest. I'm sorry, but I can't stay with you. You're gonna be safe here. I'll be back in a while. I've got the key and will lock the door. There is a bottle of whiskey on the stand, and if you need a drink, then have at it. I'm sorry that I can't stay, but I've another matter that needs tendin' to, and it can't wait."

Bass rushed out the door and down the stairs. He raced to the corral to make sure the mare was still there. Satisfied, he then raced back to the roadhouse.

He topped the porch stairs and was just entering the swinging doors when he saw English Bob at the top of the second floor stairway.

The Englishman was swearing at the top of his lungs. "What in the hell is going on in this bloody establishment? I come in here for some fun, peace and quiet, and all I hear is damn noise and bloody confusion. I bloody well had better not find out who the bastard is that disturbed my sleep."

Bass stepped through the swing doors and said, "You found 'im."

Bob looked stunned. He put his hands to his sleep-filled eyes and wiped them. He dropped them to his side when finished and said, "Bass, old boy. I never expected the pleasure of your bloody company."

Bass said, "It's obvious since you don't have your pistol. I heard you say that whoever woke you was gonna have hell to pay. I'm here to collect. Go strap on your pistol and hurry back. We got business to do."

Bob stood at the top of the stairs for a moment. He clearly was trying to figure what his next move should be. After a few moments of thought, he shrugged his shoulders, turned and walked back to the room from which he had come.

Bass stepped into the shadows, under the overhanging upstairs walkway. He could plainly see the stairs from this position, but someone at the top of the stairs would have a hard time seeing him. This man had proven to be a snake, and Bass certainly was not going to give this snake any opportunity to strike.

Bass stood for several minutes, hearing not a sound or movement from above. In the meantime, all of the men in the roadhouse made for the door and were soon well away from the building.

More minutes passed before Bass finally heard a door open. He could hear the floor above him creaking as the Englishman crept down the hall. The way he was moving told Bass that this was not going to be a face-to-face encounter.

He could follow the man's every movement by the sound of his footsteps in the upstairs walkway and from the dust that filtered through the cracks of the overhead boards. He could see the toe of Bob's boot as he started to turn the corner to enter the stairs. As he stepped down the stairs, the butt of a shotgun appeared at his thigh. He continued to cautiously move down the stairs, ever so slowly, looking from side to side.

Bass grabbed a bottle that was setting on the table next to him. He threw it, hitting the wall behind the stairs.

English Bob swung the shotgun and forced the two barrels over the banister. Bass stepped from under the overhang and into the light, saying, "Here I am!"

As Bob started to swing the barrels in that direction, Bass pulled both triggers on his pistols. The report was as if there were only one shot, but fire and flame came from both barrels. Bass knew that the projectiles had hit their mark, but his pent up hostility caused him to fire both pistols again as the Englishman dropped his shotgun and fell down the stairs head first. He came to rest at the base of the stairs, his eyes looking toward the ceiling, blood flowing from the four holes in his body as he gasped for air.

Bass had a feeling of relief, as he accomplished his mission. However, on reflection, he knew that his accomplishment would never replace what he had lost.

Chapter 9

Nancy

Bass now had completed his pursuit, bringing it to the conclusion that he had planned. The one startling thing was that he also had become involved in something that he never expected to happen.

Looking at the English man's body, recalling his own feverish pursuit of this man, realizing that none of it had come close to filling the hole in his soul, Bass came to the conclusion that if it had not been for Jane's death, he would not have been here to help Nancy. While he could not understand why Jane had been taken from him, he again believed that things happen when they happen for a reason.

Bass stepped over the Englishman and walked up the stairs. He knocked on the door where he had left Nancy and asked, "Miss Nancy, it's Bass. May I come in?"

A few moments of silence were followed by the sounds of movement, then her soft voice saying, "Yes, you have the key."

Bass used the key to open the door. The room was now very dim except for the light from the lamp on the chest across from the bed. Bass looked at the whiskey bottle and, from the lamplight shining through it, he could tell that about a fourth of it had been consumed.

Nancy was sitting on the edge of the bed. She had combed her hair and straightened her dress as best she could. Her face still was flushed, and her eyes showed that she had been crying. Now, however, she had composed herself enough to greet Bass.

"Bass, Bass, I'm so happy that you were here." She again started to sob. "I just don't know what would have happened if you had not shown up!" Again she started to sob, brushing her tears away with a piece of cloth that she evidently had torn from the sheet.

"Miss Nancy, what happened?"

"Bass, do you remember when the new troops were training at the camp, and that George Ingram and I ran off? George and I had planned to get married, or I wouldn't have run off from home. George had an uncle in Atoka, in Indian Territory. His uncle had a thriving store and needed him to come and help run it.

"George didn't want to leave without me, and I didn't want him to go without me. I knew that father would not allow me to marry him because George's dad and my dad had been bitter political enemies. In fact, he had forbidden me to even talk to him when we went to Paris."

She again started to sob and brush the tears from her face. "We got married, and George and his uncle created a great partnership. The store prospered even more, and all was going well. I guess our prosperity was so evident, however, that we became a target for robbers.

"We got held up once, and they got away with a good sum of money. You know there is no real law in the Territory, and George swore that it would never happen again. He and his uncle started carrying pistols under their aprons.

"I would come by in the afternoons and keep books for the store. Everything was going well. Then yesterday, those two bastards came in and held up the store. George and Uncle Ben both had a shootout with them, and they both got killed."

She again started to sob. This time, Bass poured some whiskey in a glass and handed it to her. She used both hands to lift it to her mouth, and between sobs, took a drink. In a few moments, she forced herself to continue her story.

"I was in the back room counting the money when all this was happening. I tried to lock the door, but they broke it down, came in and slapped me down. While they were gathering the money, they decided to take me with them. They said that they knew a place where they could sell me, and that the way I looked, I should bring a lot of money. They set the store on fire when we left for no reason except just to watch it burn. They tied me on a horse and headed here."

She again stopped and took a drink. This time she stared into the glass, as if an answer would suddenly appear.

"The next thing I know, I am being treated like a side of beef, and when the crowd cleared, I saw you standing there. I had prayed all the way here for someone to deliver me from these bastards, but I never dreamed that the same man who had saved me in Paris would be here. You just don't know how my heart jumped when I saw you."

"Well, Miss Nancy, I just don't know what to say. My lady just got killed the other day, and the shootin' you heard was me getting' a little piece of payback. I'm really sorry for your loss. I know how it hurts, but I'm also glad that I was here to help you. Now, what do you wanta do?"

"Daddy is still in the war. I have not heard from him for a long time. I hope he's all right. He wrote me that you had disappeared at the battle of Pea Ridge. He had no idea what had happened to you, but I remember him saying he sure hoped the Yankees had not killed you. He felt that he owed you a lot.

"Uncle Ben had no family. That's why he needed George to come to help him. We have some money in the bank, but it will be safe there until I return. I think I would like to go back to Atoka for a few days, and then back to Texas for a while. I just don't think that I can stand to face all the tragedy that I saw in Atoka. I do need to see that George and his uncle are laid to rest. And I must see about Louise and the house."

"Louise? Who is Louise?" Bass asked.

"She was my maid for all the time I have been in Atoka, and she has been a God-send. She has been so special to me, as well as George, and I know that she is worried something fierce about me. Of course, she could not replace your mama, but she sure is close.

"I also have some papers and clothing, along with a few items that I don't want to be without."

She paused, then looked up at him and asked, "Bass, would you take me back to my home in Texas?"

"Miss Nancy, I'm still a slave there, and I ain't 'bout to become one again. As bad as I want to help you and to see Mama, the risk is too great."

Nancy again took a drink and looked in the glass. This time she swirled the contents around as she stared into the bottom.

After another long pause, she looked up and said, "Bass, you saved me twice, and Daddy said that you saved him at least twice. If you'll take me back, I'll free you and your mama and give you two hundred dollars for a fresh start. Then the two of you can go wherever you like."

Bass stood and tried to understand what he had just heard. He shook his head, thinking he needed to come out of this dream. He then realized that he had heard the answer to his prayers. This lady whom he had known all of his life and whom he had served as a slave was now offering not only him, but to his mother, freedom, freedom to go and do as they liked. He instantly recalled when his Mama had told him that no matter what he accomplished, he would never be a man until he was free.

"Miss Nancy, I know you are tired and hurtin' somthin' fierce. Let's stay the night, and if'n you feel the same in the mornin', I'll take you home. Now, I'll lock the door and sleep outside, so you have no fear. You just relax and pull yourself together, and we'll talk in the mornin'."

As he turned to leave, Nancy said, "Bass, you're one of the best men I have ever known. I won't change my mind, so you have no fear."

Bass left the room suddenly feeling like a huge weight had been lifted from his shoulders. It was not until he turned the corner at the stairs and saw Bob laying there that he realized what had brought about all this. As great a loss as Jane was, without her loss, none of this would have taken place.

As he passed the corpse of the Englishman, he noticed the man's shotgun; the one English Bob had hoped to use to kill him. Now Bass remembered how it had glistened, even in the pale light of the roadhouse, and he understood why. The gun was more than a gun. It was a magnificent, unusual piece of artwork. He reached down and lifted it closer to his face, carefully studying the engravings set in gold on a silver inlayed stock, and the silver barrels cast with a hexagon pattern.

Only a rich Englishman could have afforded this piece of art. However, now Bass became its owner. He cradled the shotgun in his arm and pulled the pearl handled pistol from its holster. A prize of survival, he thought, remembering that he had been told that some past president had said, "To the victors goes the spoils."

The roadhouse was still empty. The events of the afternoon had seemed to take all the entertainment off the minds of those in the area.

Bass stepped out on the porch and noticed that the horse was still tied to the hitching post that the two men had used to bring Nancy here. He untied it and led it to the corral, removed the saddle and put it with the rest. He checked King and then the mare. He then fed and watered all the horses. He walked to the pile of hay and chose a comfortable place to retire for the night.

Chapter 10

Texas

Bass rose early and attended to all the horses. He took his time and re-wrapped the mare's leg before walking her around the corral and studying her condition. He decided that if they traveled slowly, he could get her to Atoka and at least leave her at the livery and have someone there take care of her.

Bass rummaged through the equipment in the barn and found the Englishman's saddle and the boot for the shotgun. He carefully placed the shotgun in the boot and placed the saddle on the horse that he had re-trieved from the front of the roadhouse. It was a fine saddle, one that made the ordinary horse look much better than it was.

He returned to the roadhouse and hurried up to Nancy's room. He did not have to knock. She already had the door open and was standing in front of the mirror, attempting to make her tattered dress look as presentable as possible.

It was an impossible task. The dress was ripped, and the straps were so torn that she could not keep them on her shoulders.

Bass said, "Miss Nancy, if you'll wait a minute, I'll see if I can help you."

He went to the room next door and knocked. After a few minutes, a woman's voice said, "Go away, I ain't workin' at this time of da mornin'."

Bass said through the door, "Lady I ain't lookin' for company. I would like to buy some of your clothes."

"What kind of sick son-of-a-bitch is you'ins? Why do they send all of you crazies to my room?"

"Lady I really want to buy some cloths. I got twenty dollars."

Bass could hear her feet hit the floor and rapidly race to the door. She fumbled with the lock for a moment, and then hurled the door open. When she stared into Bass' face, her mouth dropped and she said, "You're the nigger that kilt the Englishman. I seen it last night from my room. You run off all of my customers."

"Lady, I am sorry if I hurt your business, but the bastard killed my girl and he needed killin'. Now if you would sell me some women's clothes, I'll try to make it up to you."

She looked at him from head to toe as she rubbed her chin.

Bass was returning the appraisal, since she wasn't wearing a stitch of clothing. Obviously, the prospect of making twenty dollars motivated her to rush to the door before dressing. He finally turned his head toward the ceiling and waited for an answer.

"Hey, you know I got a bastard that owes me some money and won't pay. Would you kill 'em for me?"

"Lady, I'm sorry for you, but all I need is a dress and lady things that you might have worn to town or somethin' like that. If it is good enough, I'll give you this twenty."

She stared at the gold piece in his hand, then said, "Come over here to my wardrobe and take whatever you want."

Bass looked through the assortment and finally found a common yellow dress with some light blue flowers painted on it. He asked, "How 'bout this?"

She nodded and handed him some undergarments, then stuck out her open hand for the money.

Hurrying back to the room, he handed the clothes to Nancy and said, "I hope this stuff 'll do."

Nancy said, "It'll do fine. Now go get the horses and bring them out front. I'll meet you there in a little bit."

***

The journey to Atoka was slow. Bass saw no reason for speed. His sole concern was making sure that the mare did not aggravate her injury. He stopped everywhere there was running water, soaking her leg in hopes that it would reduce the swelling.

With all the precautions Bass was taking with the mare, it took two days to get to their destination. They had been fortunate when they found a home where the family recognized Nancy from the store. They let her spend the night in the house, while Bass slept in the barn.

In Atoka, she was met by many of her friends and store customers. All of them expressed their sympathy, and the one thing that was most on their minds — whether or not she was going to rebuild the store.

She wisely avoided telling them no. She explained that she had to go back to her home in Texas for some business, but promised she would try to return as quickly as possible. She did go to the bank and withdraw most of her funds, making sure that the banker understood that she was planning to return, but had some bills she needed to clear up in Texas before she could come back and put her energy into rebuilding the store.

Nancy rushed from the bank to her home. She swiftly pushed open the gate to the yard. She had not reached the front door when it swung open and Louise rushed out and placed a huge welcoming hug on her. Louise's eyes were full of tears, and she squeezed Nancy as if she were her long lost child.

"Lordy, Lordy, my prayers has been answered. I is so glad to see yah. I feared that I would never lay eyes on yah again. Oh my God baby, yah don't knows how much I has prayed that yah was awright, and here yah is. My prayers has been answered."

"Louise, I missed you so and was also praying that you were safe and out of harm's way. Now, what has happened in my absence?"

"Well, I still has bad news for yah. I'm sorry to say that just last night two fellers tried to break in the house. They were drunk, and I runs 'em off with the shotgun, but they stole the horses and wagon. Had 'em already hitched before they came to the house. I's think they was plannin' on takin' everthing yah had. I went this mornin' to the sheriff and tolds him 'bout it, but he didn't pay me no never mind," Louise said.

"Good Lord! I need that wagon and team. I'm going to Texas and have several things that I need to take. Do you have any idea which way they went?" Nancy asked.

"All I knows is that they headed east out of town and didn't seem to be in no great hurry."

Bass had remained in the saddle, calmly listening to the women talking in the front yard.

At the right time, he asked, "What do the horses look like?"

Nancy, glad to be reminded that he was still there, turned toward him and said, "They are a matched team of bays, and the wagon is black with red paint that reads General Store."

"Well, Miss Nancy, get your stuff settled, and I'll put the mare in the corral. If I'm lucky, I'll go and see if I can get your team back."

"Do you think you can do that?"

"Well, if they aren't movin' fast and they were drinkin', I should be able to catch 'em before night comes on," Bass said.

"Bass, that would be wonderful. If it takes you longer, I will care for the mare. I know how much you think of her, so don't worry about her," Nancy promised.

***

Bass made sure that there was plenty of water in the corral and fed the mare before mounting. He spent time studying the fresh horse and wagon tracks that led from the corral. When he had a clear picture in his mind of all the possible clues, he turned and headed east.

In spite of all of the other traffic that had gone down the road, it was easy for him to follow the wagon and team, as the right-hand horse was shy a shoe on its right front hoof, and the left-hand horse was shy a shoe on its right rear hoof.

These clues made the tracking easy, and with Bass's keen eye, he was able to move at a surprisingly rapid pace.

About three hours into the pursuit, he was relieved to see that the wagon had left the road and headed toward a grove of trees. From his position, he could see that both men now were lying under the wagon with a jug between their prone bodies.

Bass approached and dismounted. He slowly walked to the sleeping thieves before squatting down to observe them in their deep drunken sleep. He reached up and removed their pistols, then took a stick and poked both of them violently in their ribs.

Both men grunted and then sat up. As they did, one of them struck his head on the bottom of the wagon and let out a mighty curse as he grabbed his head.

As they tried to compose themselves, Bass asked, "You fellers know what they do to horse thieves in this territory?"

"We didn't steal no horses," one of the men said defiantly. "These are us'ins."

"Really? I guess you has some papers to prove that?" Bass played along.

Both men looked at the other, and then acted like they were searching their pockets for papers. One then went for his holster, surprised to find it vacant.

Bass held up the man's pistol. "Guess your lookin' for this?"

"No, no, I was just hopin' that the papers were in my britches pocket here," the man tried to say convincingly.

Bass said, "You know, I could give you all day, and you couldn't come up with the papers 'cause you stole this rig last night from my friend's corral. I'm not goin' to hang you, like I should, but I am gonna take you back to the sheriff and see what he might do to you."

Bass secured both men in the back of the wagon. He tied King behind the wagon, and then began driving the trip back to Atoka where he placed both men in the custody of the sheriff.

When he reached Miss Nancy's house the flickering lamplight was shining through the window. He knocked on the door and was greeted by a surprised Louise.

"Yah is back awready?" she said, ushering him into the house where Nancy was sitting.

"It was not that hard to track two drunks, and they helped in that they decided to take a nap on the trail.

"Miss Nancy, we has to get the team shod before we go on the trip. It was a blessing that they were in need 'cause it made the trailin' simple, but we can't go till that is done."

Nancy said, "While you were gone, I found a livery man, who all say is as good a horse doctor as there is in these parts and was assured that he could provide great care for the mare. He is located next to the blacksmith, and they say he has a really nice pasture where the mare can rest and get the time to heal."

"That's great news," Bass said. "I'll get that done in the mornin'. I know you have the funeral to take care of, and it will give me time to do what I have to do."

***

The burial of George and his uncle was a well-attended affair. They were probably the most well known people in town. When the service was over, the sheriff asked Nancy several questions and got the description of the two killers. He promised that he would track them down, but Nancy knew that he was just being nice to her. There was no way he was going to spend his time or effort away from the poker game that he ran on the side.

Bass took the mare and team to the livery stable. While the blacksmith did his job, Bass visited with the livery owner. The owner promised he would treat the mare every day that she was left in the livery, which was a great relief to Bass. Bass even took great solace in the fact that the two men felt sure the mare would regain use of most of her leg and probably live a normal life. However, she would never be the speed horse she once was. There was no reason, however, why she could not be used for a breeding mare and, after examining her, the livery owner said the mare already had had at least one colt and surely could have more.

Bass paid for the mare's care for the next twenty days, with the assurance that if he was detained and the bill grew larger, he would pay more when he returned.

***

Bass, Louise and Nancy loaded the wagon before heading south toward the Red River. It took several days for the journey, but they were prepared for the trip. On nights when they couldn't find lodging, Bass would pitch a tent and use the wagon for shelter.

The evening hours were spent visiting about what each had done since they had last seen each other. No matter what they talked of, the conversation always went back to the time Bass and Nancy had spent on the Reeves' farm.

However, as they approached the ferry to cross the Red River, Bass became more anxious than he could remember. He had dreamed of seeing his mother many times, and he had hoped the war would end before something bad happened to her. He couldn't wait to hug her again.

The ferry seemed like it would never reach the Texas bank. As soon as the travelers were ashore, their speed increased. Nancy wanted to see the place that had meant so much to her growing up, and Bass became even more excited to see Mama with every mile they traveled.

Chapter 11

Mama

The approach to the Reeves' farm was exciting for both Bass and Nancy. They both had been away for some time, and it seemed that most of the things they observed had reminiscences associated with them.

Bass basically reflected on his work and how it had taught him to be self-reliant. But his most memorable thoughts, outside of the warmth and comfort of his mother, were of his learning about guns and their power. These memories were nearly equaled by his work with horses.

Nancy's thoughts related to her childhood recollections of home, her Papa and the carefree life she had enjoyed. Her most memorable experiences were of George and how he and she had met so many times with the cover of night, ultimately leading to their running away to Indian Territory to get married.

Bass and Nancy shared the recollection of the creek, that first time that Bass had been more than a mere servant to Nancy. Even though they had their horses in a more rapid gait, they could not help but discuss that day when Bass had used his courage and strength to pull Nancy and her friend Alice to safety.

Nancy smiled at the memory, saying, "Bass, that was the first day that I realized that you were a man and an important part of the life that I had been living. It was some feat of strength that you displayed when you pulled us both from the creek and carried Alice on your back to the house. Alice must have weighed at least ten pounds more than you, and yet you carried her at least a quarter of a mile."

"Miss Nancy, all I did is what I thought needed doin'."

"Well, it left an impression on me and a feeling of indebtedness to you. The fact that you also saved me from being molested by that drunk in Paris and so calmly went to jail with the possibility of being hanged was very impressive. Little did I know that in the future I would have even more need of your help, and that you would come through for me. All I can say is that you have been the answer to my prayers more than once."

"Miss Nancy, Mama always told me and now I believe it, that everythin' has a reason, and while they may not be understood at the time, they will show themselves in a way you never expect. After that time in Paris, I told Mama when I got back home that my only real fear was that I might not see her again. But I knew that I had done the right thing, and you always has to do the right thing. If you don't, you ain't doin' what you was placed here for."

When they got on the property, Bass began noticing how many acres were being cultivated. This greatly puzzled him. He and the other slaves had worked full time, and they never were able to get anywhere near this amount of ground in production. He had heard that the war had caused a great shortage of food, so he concluded that part of the place must be leased out to others.

While he was thinking about it, he asked Nancy who was in charge of the farm now.

"My cousin Joe," she said. "A horse fell on him so he couldn't enlist because he was injured, the accident worked out just perfect for Papa. Joe couldn't go to war, and Papa needed a man to run this place.

"Why?" she asked.

"Well, it just looks like there sure has been a lot of work done, so I was just wonderin'," Bass said.

They slowed their horses as they came to the back of the barn, and then put them in a walk. When they rounded the corral they eyed the place to see the changes, before they stopped, dismounted and tied their horses to the corral.

Bass was staring at the quarters, and even from this distance he could smell Mama's cooking. It had been so long since he had known these smells that he just stood and thought for a moment.

For some reason, he wanted to feel free and relaxed as he breathed in the air, so he unbuckled his pistols and pulled his rifle from its boot.

"Miss Nancy, could I bother you and Louise to take these to the house? It just don't seem fittin' that I have 'em on when I goes to see Mama."

Nancy reached out to take them and smiled. "I think you are exactly right. You need to look like the boy that left, not the man that has come back."

Bass stood and watched as Nancy and Louise walked toward the house. He was trying to gather his thoughts before he went to the quarters. He was starting to laugh at himself, all of the things he had faced with no second thoughts, and now he seemed to be apprehensive about seeing his mother.

He quickly was brought out of his hesitation by a noise coming from the barn. He knew it wasn't the sound of horses, though it sounded like horses pulling against traces and the clattering of chains that goes with it. The noise was followed by the sound of people talking.

He turned and started toward the door, again hearing voices coming from the enclosure.

Slowly he pulled the doors open, letting in more and more light as he pulled them further and further apart. He slowly stepped inside and was greeted by twenty sets of eyes staring at him.

"Who are you, and what are you doin' here?"

His question was followed by silence. The only response he got was twenty black heads looking from side to side.

"I said, who are you, and what you doin' here?"

One of the strangers said, "We is slaves, and we sleep here. Who is you?"

"I'm Bass Reeves, and my mama is the cook here."

Smiles instantly started encompassing the faces of those who were observing him, and the one who had spoken started to slowly walk toward him. His pace was slow, because he was wearing an ankle chain that was causing the person attached to him to have to follow.

"You'd better get outta here before Lucas gets back. You'll be in a heap of trouble if he finds yah here. We has heard 'bout yah so much from yah mama, and we knows yah is a brave man, but yah is in real trouble here."

"I doubt that. I'm here with Miss Nancy. But why are you in chains? Workers here have never been chained."

"We is the ones that Lucas don't trust. Most of us has tried to escape from times to times, and Lucas keeps us chained in the barn or workin' in the field. He is one bad man. He whipped my friend to death a while back for not doin' what he wanted done fast enough, and none of use ain't escaped his beatins. Yah don't understand. Master Lucas takes care of all the slaves and the story we heard is that yah is one of us."

"Who is this Lucas feller?"

"He is the foreman here for Master Joe, and he is one mean man. He loves to beat on us and makes us feel like animals. He is really bad when he has been drinkin', and this is Sunday, and he and Master Joe always goes to Paris and spends their Saturday night and Sunday drinkin'. When he comes back, we all has to pay a price. We was afraid that yah was him when we heard yah ride up."

Bass said, "I think you is gonna find that there is 'bout to be some changes here. You all should just relax. I'll come back and visit you in a while, but right now I has to go and see my Mama."

By now, Bass had shed all of his apprehension. All he wanted to do now was see his mother and make sure that all was well. But these new findings filled his head with thoughts that he had never imagined.

Stepping into his Mama's quarters, he stared into the darkened kitchen and saw his mother bent over a large pot, stirring it and adding things as she hummed.

Bass softly said, "Mama, your boy is home."

Mama turned with the large spoon still in her hand. Her mouth dropped at the same time as her hand with the spoon fell to her side. She slowly started walking toward Bass, a smile starting to spread across her face as her eyes lit up.

She let out what was supposed to be a greeting, but it sounded more like a scream. "Good Lord. Good Lord. My prayers have been answered."

She now started running, rushing to throw her arms around Bass' neck, still holding the huge spoon in her hand.

Bass pulled her to him, and they swayed as they held each other. After several minutes, Bass pushed her back and placed a kiss on her cheek, and then pulled her back into him with his massive grasp. They again swayed in each other's arms, and Mama spoke again, "Child, child, I've missed yah so. I've prayed that yah was safe, and I've wanted to hold yah so bad. Thank God yah is here and safe."

After an extended time of hugs and kisses, Bass said, "Let me looks at you. I've dreamed of you, and I just wanta make sure I is really with you."

Bass pushed her back to arm's length and held her there. He was so pleased to see her, and he was amazed at how she had not seemed to have changed. The only thing he noticed was that her left cheek seemed to be swollen and dark.

"What happened to your face?"

"Bass, nothin'. I just fell the other day and hit my cheek on the edge of the table. It's nothin'. I'm so glad yah is here. Let's set and talk. Tell me all about where yah been and what yah been doin'."

Bass started to relay the stories about the war, Indian Territory and the Mankillers. He went into great detail about Jane and how he had lost her. While he was talking, a young girl came in and sat beside the pair. She never spoke, just listened intently.

Mama finally noticed her and said, "Bass, this is Jennie. She helps me in the kitchen and is my best friend. She is one super girl and knows all 'bout yah. I has told her stories 'bout yah so many times she is probably sick of hearin' 'em."

Jennie said, "No, Mama, I just loves to hear 'em, and now I see the man that they is 'bout, so jest keep on talkin'."

Hours passed, and Bass still was telling stories when Jennie suddenly jumped up and rushed toward the door. She had been sitting where she could see who was approaching the house. She shouted, "My God, Lucas and Master Joe has just rode up. Bass, yah had better hide. Bass, he is a mean man, and if he finds yah here, he'll be really snortin' mad, and when he is drinkin', he is really mean."

Bass said, "I have seen the men in the barn, and it don't seem fitin'. They have told me stories, and this just ain't right. Something is gonna have to change around here, and it is gonna have to be soon.

"Mama, in all this excitement, I forgot to tell you that I brought Miss Nancy back," Bass said. "She is in the house, so I have nothin' to fear. She is gonna free me and you."

"She is what? Did yah say she was gonna free us?" Mama asked.

"Mama, she promised me that if I did some things for her, she would free both of us."

"Good Lord, what a day. The two things I want most in the world is happenin' on the same day. No wonder it's a Sunday. The Lord has sure come to visit today," Mama said.

Jennie said, "She may of told yah that, but yah better not believe it. Lucas is one mean and powerful man, and I can't see him lettin' anything keep him from doin' as he wants. That bruise on yah mama's cheek is jest one of his shows of what he'll do to get what he wants. I can tell yah more---but that's my story."

Bass was now standing and looking at his mother's face. His eyes narrowed, and his jaw tightened.

"Why did you lie to me, Mama?"

"Bass, I is not hurt, and I don't want no trouble. This is a day for happiness. Let it pass."

Standing, Bass looked taller than he had on his entrance. He started to the door, stopped and put his hand on the doorjam as he stared toward the house. He felt his sides, remembering he was without his weapons.

While he was looking at the house, Nancy rushed out and onto the porch, shouting, "Bass, come here I need you!"

He noticed that she had one of his pistols in her hand, so he knew there was trouble.

Bass immediately pushed himself through the door and briskly started to walk toward the big house.

He had gone no more than four steps into his journey when a big man pushed his way by Nancy, knocking her to the ground, before starting toward Bass.

As he was walking, he said, "I guess you is the black son-of-a-bitch that I have heard so much about. Well, you is gonna learn that you is still a slave and still belong to this property."

As he was speaking, he let the coil of a bullwhip attached to his wrist unfold from his right hand. He flipped the whip to its full length and watched as it hit the ground.

He then looked toward Bass, and said, "Now, nigger, I'm tellin' you to get to the barn where you belong."

As this was happening, Joe rushed from the house, past where Nancy was struggling to get to her feet, intent on watching his man teach a resister a lesson. Before Joe realized it, however, Nancy had gained her footing and picked the pistol from the ground.

Bass said, "I'm afraid you is confused. I don't take orders from no one and especially someone what likes to beat on women. You hit Mama, and you hit Miss Nancy, and you is gonna have to pay for that."

Before he had finished speaking, Lucas had pulled the whip back and brought it forward with full force.

The cracker flew through the air, and Lucas pulled back just as it reached Bass' body. The whip tore into Bass' left shoulder.

The pain was unbelievable. Bass had never felt anything like it. He knew that he could not stand this attack for long and decided that the only good defense was a rapid offense.

Joe was so intent on Lucas and Bass that he did not realize that Nancy was now on her feet with the pistol pointed squarely at his back.

Lucas seemed to enjoy watching Bass' face, and said, "Now, nigger, do you understand what is gonna happen to you if you don't get to the barn?"

Blood was running down Bass' arm, and he was stooped over and grasping the painful wound.

Lucas drew the whip back, but the moment he stepped forward, Bass rushed directly toward him. The length of the whip went past Bass, but his quick hands clutched the extended leather. The move had not spared him the pain, for the cracker still hit him in the side and back. The pain again was intense, but Bass knew that he had to hold onto the whip with all of his strength and determination.

He finally gained some of his footing and pulled with all of his might against the leather attached to Lucas' wrist. This jerked first Lucas' arm, then his whole body forward, causing him to lose his balance and begin stumbling.

As Lucas' now out of control body neared, Bass lunged forward with his right shoulder and caught Lucas in the stomach. Bass wrapped his right arm around Lucas' body and hoisted him into the air. Bass took three steps forward and slammed the big man to the ground.

The sound of the air leaving Lucas' body was akin to steam leaving a locomotive. Bass positioned himself in the middle of the man's stomach and immediately struck Lucas in the left side of the face with his huge right fist. He struck him again and again until the side of his face was covered with blood. His last release saw teeth flying from Lucas' mouth while his nose bent to his right.

Joe started to step from the porch to assist his man when he felt the point of the pistol barrel slam into his back, at the same time hearing the cylinder roll and the hammer cock.

Nancy said in a calm voice, "If you take one step, I will end your miserable life right here and now."

Bass staggered to his feet. He took the whip and wrapped it twice around Lucas' neck, then stepped over the prone man and started to drag him across the yard.

"Bass, stop that! Stop that right now! You can kill him, and that'd ruin all of your hopes for you and your mom's freedom," Nancy shouted. "Let him go and come in the house. I've got problems of my own, and I need you in here."

Her words caused Bass to halt his attack, but he was not satisfied. He reached down and totally picked the big man off the ground. He carried him to the horse tank, hoisted him in the air and threw him in.

Bass reached down and pushed the man's face down in the water. He held it there momentarily, and then abruptly pulled it up. He did this several times until Lucas started gasping for air and commenced resisting.

Now that Bass had the man conscious, he lifted Lucas to his feet and pushed him out of the tank.

Lucas stumbled and fell to the ground. Bass picked up the whip and struck him while he was lying on the ground. "You got ten seconds to get to your feet or I am gonna hit you again."

There was a stream of blood coming from the rip in Lucas' shirt where he had been struck.

Lucas struggled to get to his feet. He was not able to get his balance, so Bass kicked him with great force in his elevated ass.

Lucas continued to try to crawl and Bass continued to apply his boot. After several kicks, Bass reached down and jerked him to his feet.

"I am sorry I have to go, but I sure don't want you to be lonely."

Bass dragged him to the barn door and as he pushed him through it, said, "There are some friends of yours in here that I thinks would like to get better acquainted with you."

Bass turned and hurried toward the house. When he entered, Nancy had total control of Joe, who was sitting in a chair.

"Bass, this low life has stolen money from me and my papa and has turned this place into a house of horror. It did not take me but a moment to discover this by looking at the books," Nancy said. "When I showed him the papers that Papa gave me to allow me total control of his property any time I wanted to return, this disgusting bastard tried to take them from me. If I hadn't had your pistol, I think he would have done it.

"This farm has always been a place of honor and respect, and the people have been treated fairly. How this bastard has turned it into a place of shame sickens me, and I will not stand for it. I want him off this property and out of my life forever. Can you see to that?" she asked Bass.

"Yes, Miss Nancy, it will be my pleasure."

Bass reached out his right hand, grabbed Joe by the throat and bodily lifted him to his feet.

Using both of his hands, Joe grabbed Bass' hand and struggled for freedom, but to no avail. Bass now had both of Joe's feet off the floor as he carried him toward the door.

Once outside, Bass threw the man across the porch toward where the horses were tied.

Joe hit the ground and rolled, but did not get to his feet immediately as he was struggling to get air back into his lungs. He finally coughed and gasped until he had some semblance of relief.

Bass then lifted him to his feet and handed him the reins of both horses.

"I think you had better hurry," Bass said. "Your man is in the barn, and I think that his party may be gettin' out of hand. If you don't hurry, you're probably gonna have to ride alone."

Joe hurried to the barn. However, he did not exit like Bass had expected. After a few minutes, Bass rushed to the barn.

He entered just in time to witness the gang of slaves releasing their leg chains from around the throats of the two hated enslavers.

Bass stood for a moment and realized how foolish he had been sending these two into this den of hatred.

He slowly thought, and then asked, "Where are the keys to your chains?"

"Lucas kept 'em in the house is all I know," one of the men said.

"Well, I guess I had better go and get 'em. Just stay calm, and I'll return."

As Bass walked toward the house, he was filled with concern. He would have to explain this to Nancy and put a plan in motion to resolve the incident.

As Bass entered the house, he was greeted by Nancy who was sitting in her father's chair; her eyes were full of tears that she slowly wiped away as they rolled down her face.

Nancy said, "You know, I wish I had killed Joe rather than let him go. He signed a release at gunpoint, but what he has done to my memories of this place cannot be forgotten or forgiven."

"Well, if that's what you wanted, then it has been taken care of," Bass said. "What do you mean?"

"Well, the men in the barn did what you just wished," Bass said.

"Really?" she asked, bewildered and slightly frightened.

"Yes. It was my fault. I never should've put those two in the barn with those men, but what is done is done. I'll have the men bury the two out in the fields later tonight, and all you have to do is tell some of the people in town that they left, and you have no idea where they went."

Nancy thought for a moment, and then let out a great sigh. "Good riddance. We will do as you say. I have no remorse."

Now, I need the keys to the chains. Do you have any idea where they may be?"

"It must be those hanging over there by the door. Take them and get on with what needs to be done."

Bass took the keys and went to the barn. He was gone several minutes, and then returned to the main house.

Nancy observed him carefully, noticing that he was still holding his shoulder. "Bass are you hurt?"

"Not bad, Miss Nancy. I'll be alright."

"Let's get you to the kitchen, and let Mama have a look at you."

Bass said, "That's what we should do, but before we go, I'd like to have my pistols. None of these things would have happened like they did if I hadn't give them to you in the first place."

"Wise thoughts but if I hadn't had them, things probably would have been worse," she said. "Still, I'll get them for you."

Nancy returned with his pistols, and Bass buckled his usual companions around his waist. They had been a part of him for so long now that he could not believe he had sent them to the house with Nancy.

On the trip to the quarters, Bass held his shoulder and felt the blood that had soaked his ripped shirt. He never had felt the lash, and it was more intense than he had ever imagined. The sting seemed like it would never subside. The pain in his side was as if he had been kicked by a mule, then set on fire. He now understood why so many of the slaves he had visited with over the years had a real commitment to never feel the master's displeasure again.

Bass rubbed his arm as he walked, hoping the motion would bring back some of the natural feeling. On the journey, he removed his shirt and looked at the long streak of red. The center of the streak was the source of blood, but the entire area was swollen as if he had been stung by a hive of bees.

He observed his side, as best he could, and again found a red streak that was much wider. It looked more like he had been hit with a club, and the swelling looked as if it might erupt at any moment. He knew that the chances of him ever getting these sorts of wounds were much lessened with the demise of Lucas and Joe, and he was relieved that the two could no longer inflict their misery on others.

Mama came rushing out of the kitchen area as he approached and immediately took his left arm to look at the nasty work that the black snake had done to her boy.

"Child gets to the kitchen. I needs to wash that and put some medicine on it. Some cool water will makes it feel better."

She led him to the kitchen as if he were unable to make the journey himself. It reminded him of how long it had been since he had felt his mother's touch. There was nothing like the care of his mother in the time of pain and discomfort.

Mama and Jennie fussed over him like he was a newborn child, and he figured that in their minds, he was somewhat of a new project and one that his mother felt she had to comfort.

Mama said, "I was so scared. Child, I was 'fraid yah jest got here and was gonna get kilt. Praise the Lord, yah is OK. Now, set down here and let me looks at that arm."

While Mama was working to stop the bleeding, she was visiting with Nancy. Nancy told of her recent misfortunes at Atoka, and how Bass had once again saved her from more humiliation than she could imagine. It was at this moment that she repeated her promise to free both Bass and Mama as soon as she could get the paperwork completed.

"Oh, Miss Nancy yah is a angel. All my life I has dreamed of freedom," Mama said. "I has spent so many years of my life workin' here and takin' care of all these men. I jest hopes I can get accustomed to all the new things."

Nancy said, "That reminds me. Where are Ned and the others who have been here all of these years."

Mama told her that they had gone to the creek to bathe and try to catch some fish for the table.

"Well, when they get back have Ned come to the house. I have some things I want him to do for me, and, on top of that, I would like some time to visit with him.

"Mama, I am going to be here for a while. I know you need time with your boy, so let's plan on getting together later. I want breakfast early in the morning. I have to get to town and take care of some urgent business."

With that, she prepared to leave, telling Bass, "Once again, Bass, my thanks to you. I know I'm leaving you now in good hands."

Chapter 12

At Last

As Mama and Jennie continued to clean and bandage Bass' wounds, Bass thought it seemed a good time for more stories of his life over the past few years. Of course, the more stories he told, the more questions he had to answer.

Mama finally interrupted and, with a proud smile on her face, said, "Bass, first I gotta tell yah that yah is now a man. I seen yah do things today that I never thought I woulda seen. I's remember tellin' yah that yah ain't a man till yah acted like a man, and I has great pride in what yah done today. If I ever saw a man doin' what he was supposed to do, today was the day. I only wish yah papa coulda seen yah. I know he woulda been struttin' 'is stuff today, just watchin' yah.

"Those no goods had turned this place into a place of pain and misery, and now they is gone. It took a man to do that, and I is so proud that my child was the one that put them off a this place."

"Well, they're sure gone," Bass said. "And, I promise they will not bother others again. Mama, I'm just sorry that I didn't get here sooner. I am really hatin' it that you and the rest of the people here had to suffer all this time. I had wondered what your life was like here, with me and the Colonel gone, but for some reason I hadn't pictured it as a troublesome time.

"You know I'd a been here earlier if I hadda known that you was bein' mistreated, even if I woulda thought that I might lose my freedom again.

"Mama, I really missed you and thought about you nearly every day. I hope that I can make it up to you in the comin' times, and if Miss Nancy does what she has promised, I sure will."

Mama reached down and picked up the whiskey jug that Miss Nancy wisely had brought with her. Passing it to Bass, Mama said, "While I is workin' on yah, yah might as well have a pull on this. I know those lashes bit deep, and about the only thing that stops the pain is time and a good hit on this jug."

"I try not to take much of those kinds of liquids," Bass said. "I have been around Sam so long that it has really become a part of my life to stay far away from that stuff. Sam really believes that it is the devil at work. He has seen so many of his tribe and others pass from great men into nothing but empty shells. It is the cause of so many problems, and he preaches about it all the time.

"The pain will pass, and I think I will just bear it now, but thank you for your concern," Bass said.

"That Sam must be one powerful man, and I is so glad that yah got hooked up with 'im," Mama said.

"Mama, he is like my brother, and we have made some great changes in his home place, and I know he will welcome you with open arms."

Back to business, Mama said, "Now let's me see yah's arm and side. I's wanta make sure I gots yah in as good a shape as I can."

The tone in her voice left little doubt that she intended to look at his arm and side even if Bass didn't want her to. It had been a while since he had been talked to with such authority, and while it made him somewhat uncomfortable, it was welcomed coming from his Mama.

"Lordy, I was so scared yah was gonna kill that Lucas, and if'n yah had, we woulda been in a heap of trouble," Mama said as she continued with her nursing skills.

"Mama, it all worked out like it was supposed to. You always said that, and you has always been right. Miss Nancy probably came out at the right time with one of my gun. I don't know what made me give her my guns like that, but I guess the Lord had somethin' to do with it. All of these things just went together. So don't worry none now. All is taken care of."

While they talked, Mama probed and turned him to pick up the best light. Then she reached for the Master's whiskey jug and poured some of it carefully on a cloth. She swabbed and cleaned the huge marks on Bass' side and back, all the time saying, "My-oh-my." She paid special attention to his left arm. It had a gash in it as if made by a knife.

She tore more cloth, and again soaked it in the whiskey and gently bandaged the wounds. As she worked, tears appeared in her eyes before she finally broke into uncontrollable crying.

"Mama, I's not hurt that bad," Bass said, trying to comfort her.

"I's know, but this day has been so full of stuff that I jest can't helps myself. I's seen my baby, and I's gonna get my freedom, and my baby's nearly got hisself kilt, and I jest is full of feelins that I ain't had since I was took from yah's Papa. It's jest a unbelievable day and, all in all, I jest needs some relief."

"Well, Mama, hows 'bout laughin' or dancin'? You do that well."

With those words, a smile broke out on Mama's face and everyone started to laugh. Each had received a turning point in their life that day, and the emotions were indeed high.

Later, Ned came into Mama's kitchen, so he and Bass headed to the house to meet with Nancy. She told them that she was going to town the next morning, and that she wanted Ned to take her.

"I would like for Bass to go, but I'm afraid that it might cause some problems," Nancy said. "I know it has been a while since he shot that bastard in town, when he tried to attack me, but some of his friends might see Bass and there could be some real trouble if that happened. You know that the Judge's order said that you were never to return to town, and I sure wouldn't like for a small thing like that to ruin so many peoples' futures. Now, if General Maxey or the sheriff were still there, I would feel somewhat more secure, but I know that they are still in the war, just like Papa. With those two gone, I just don't want to take any chances."

Bass said, "I don't think you should go to Paris tomorrow. I just don't feel right about it."

"Bass, I have some things I must do, and I am so committed to doing them that I don't want to waste a day. Besides, I have to tell some of the people in town that Lucas and Joe are gone, and that they did not say where they were going. The more people I tell, the better it will be."

"Miss Nancy, take a pistol along with a shotgun with you. Is better to have it and not need it, than need it and not have it. You know that the shotgun is a great weapon, but you could use a backup."

She thought a moment and said, "Bass, I would be a fool not to take your advice. Go get me a couple of pistols and load them for me.

"Oh yes, and I will send Louise to help Mama for the day. I want her to learn everything there is to know about this place. She is going to stay with me and help me run this operation. So, please tell Mama that she should be expecting her."

Chapter 13

The Great Day

Nancy and Ned left early the next morning for Paris. Before leaving, Nancy again told Bass she wished he was coming with her, but she couldn't take the chance of losing him.

Bass remained hesitant for her to go, but made Ned swear that he would protect her with his life.

Later that evening, Nancy returned. As soon as he saw her approaching, Bass knew that her trip had been uneventful. Arriving, she immediately told Bass to get all of the workers and to come to the house.

Bass was curious, but he got busy gathering the workers. He couldn't help but notice that Ned's face was nothing but one huge smile. Bass asked Ned several times what was happening, but could get no response. Ned would only say, "This is goin' to be a great day."

The workers gathered on the front porch where Nancy had placed several lamps. They all stood in silence.

Nancy finally came out on the porch and said, "I have been away for far too long, and I find that things have changed greatly here at the farm. In my absence, cruelty and abuse has occurred that, even in my young days, I would not have tolerated.

"While I was away, I experienced several things that changed my feelings about the situation all of you have found yourselves in. I have decided to make up for all the wrong that has been done.

"Fortunately, my cousin, while tolerating these abuses, also ran a very prosperous farm, and probably because I showed up unannounced, he failed to withdraw the money he had probably planned on stealing.

"So, here is what I have decided to do. I not only am setting Bass and Mama free, but I also have the paper work to free all of you."

This announcement sent mumbles of excitement through the gathering. It was obvious that some were explaining the announcement to the others, and that most were having a difficult time grasping what they had heard.

Nancy realized that this news surely was hard for them to understand, so she repeated it.

"I am officially freeing all of you. Now let me finish. I also am offering all of you jobs here on the farm for as long as you like. I will furnish you food, clothing and shelter along with a living wage. You have worked well and have helped make this place profitable, far more than you can imagine. It is only fair and right that I repay you. I know that most of you have no family and no place to go, so my offer takes care of this problem. I also promise to keep you safe and comfortable as long as you work for me.

"Now, as far as Jennie is concerned, I know that she wants to go with Mama and Bass, and I happened to run into Mrs. Beasley, one of the best cooks in Paris. It seems that her husband has died, and she is in desperate shape. She has agreed to come here with her daughter and provide all the cooking and to take care of the things that Mama has done for so many years. So, you will be well cared for in spite of Mama's leaving. I know that you need to think about this for a while. I also might add, Ned will be the foreman here, and all of your dealings will be with him.

"Now go to your quarters and think of what I have said. I would like an answer from you by tomorrow."

As the group slowly left, it was apparent that the further they walked, the happier they got. By the time they were to their living quarters, laughter and shouting were echoing off all the walls.

Bass stayed with Miss Nancy while the others departed. He obviously was as shocked as those that had left for their quarters, who were now dancing and singing around a roaring camp fire.

"Miss Nancy, how can you afford to do that?" Bass asked.

"Bass, it was a simple decision. Because of the war, with so many men being gone, the profits from this expanded farm have been great. I also had quite a lot of money that I withdrew from the bank in Atoka. I didn't tell you because I didn't want you fretting and worrying when we were coming back. I have no desire to return to Atoka — this is my home. I think that if I treat these people right, I can keep the farm in a highly profitable position."

"But, some of these people were just bought, and that musta cost lots of money."

"Bass, the people that sold them knew that slavery was coming to an end, so they sold them for very little money. They figured that whatever money they got was money that they weren't gonna have anyway. On top of that, I have no thoughts that the South is going to win the war, so they would have been officially freed anyway. I just did it legal, and earlier than what would have happened anyhow.

"I also had a small taste of what the loss of freedom feels like, including the terror of not knowing what my future would be. I don't want to be a part of anything like that.

"I want you to go and make Mama as happy and comfortable as possible. I also have one last request. I know this may sound strange after what I have said, but I am giving you five hundred dollars on top of the two hundred I've already promised you. I want your promise that you will try to find those two bastards that killed my husband and uncle. I want them brought to justice anyway that you can do it. There is no man that I would trust to do this more than you, and I know that you will take the time and effort to see that it is done. There is no time limit. All I want is that it is done," she said, looking him straight in the eye with fierce determination.

"Miss Nancy, I'll do as you ask, and truly, you don't have to pay me. I had 'em in my sights once and gave 'em a chance to change their ways. If'n I had finished 'em then, none of that woulda happened to you and your husband. I's kinda feels at fault for what happened to you," Bass apologized.

"Bass, I owe you for my life, and this is only a small way that I can make it up to you. I can afford it, and I know you will need funds to set Mama up in a new home, and I also feel that I owe her for her many kindnesses that she provided me after my mother died. Both of you were an important part of my life, and I will feel good knowing that I might have made you a little happier. Besides, I want those two to pay for what they did, and I know that you can do that for me.

"Come by when you are ready to leave, and I will gladly give you the money. I also want you to know that you and Mama will be missed, and you will always be welcome back here any time you want."

Bass lowered his head and said, "You know, you has made me very happy. My Mama bein' with me has been a dream. I've felt bad that I hadn't come for her earlier. I just feel blessed that she's well and able to go with me. I thank you and promise that I'll do my best to bring 'em fellers to justice, just as soon as I get Mama settled."

Chapter 14

Settling Down

"Mama, can you ride a horse?" Bass asked.

"Well, I never done that before, but if'n it's the only way I can gets my freedom, I sure'll try."

"How 'bout you Jennie?" Bass asked, looking to the young woman.

"My answer is the exact same as your mama's," Jennie said.

"Well, I bought the two gentlest horses Miss Nancy had, and we'll take it slow," Bass promised the two women, who were looking concerned. "You didn't have much to carry, so I only bought one pack horse. You'll get your butts used to the saddle long before we're back to the Cherokee Nation."

The pace of the trip was slow, just as Bass had promised, and Mama and Jennie slowly gained confidence and skill in the saddle.

From time to time, they would pass Indian families on the trail. Mama and Jennie were totally taken by the dress and demeanor of those families they passed. The one thing that stood out, though, was how the men walked in front, and the women seemed to be carrying most of the packs or supplies. While they had been slaves, they knew that they had to do whatever chore was assigned, but they had seen enough of free women to know that this kind of responsibility was not normal in the white man's world.

Mama and Jennie were impressed that Bass could speak with most of those they met, and how he seemed to be so well respected by most everyone. They felt that they were in the company of someone who had accomplished something. It made them feel very proud.

As they traveled, Bass would take the time to visit with both Mama and Jennie, and once they had become used to the sway and bounce of their mounts, they became more relaxed and talkative themselves.

One day Bass asked, "Jennie how old are you?"

"I's think I's fourteen, but I don't rightly know. I's do knows that my mama told me when they tooks me from her that I was eight, but I really can't recall exactly when's that was."

"What do you think about goin' to Indian Territory?" he asked.

"Bass, I just wants to get out of where I was. Do yah knows that I've been a captive all of my life? My mama and papa were captives all of their lives, and I'm sure hankering for a taste of freedom. I have seen places when they brought me from Missouri, and I wondered what the people was doin' that had a choice, as we went through those towns. All I wants to do is suck in some open air and know that if'n I wants, I can walk some place or set some place or do anything I's wants."

"Jennie, you will have your freedom, but it's not quite that easy. The country where we're goin' is full of danger — far more danger than you faced at the farm. But I promise you that the danger is well worth the feeling of freedom."

"Bass, facin' Lucas every day was worse than you know, and I would trade the things I's had to do there for lots of danger. Besides, I know that yah is a good man, and if'ns it's possible, yah will take care of me. Yah mama has told me too many stories about yah for me not to believe that."

"You gotta remember that stories is stories, and all I do is try my best to be the best I can be. I know you heard my stories when I was talkin' to Mama, but I'm only one man, and there are many challenges ahead of us," Bass cautioned.

"Again, all I wants is a chance to be free, and I is willin' to take that chance with yah and Mama. I don't think that I's can face much more danger than I's already faced, and I's survived that. I is strong, and I has made up my mind to make somthin' with my freedom."

"Tis a good mind set you've got," Bass said. "It should get you a long way."

Finally, the trio made it to Atoka. As they rode down the street, they felt the eyes of the town following them. It was probably good that several people on the street remembered Bass from his accompanying

Miss Nancy.

The stares did not matter to Bass. He only wanted to pick up the mare and get on his way. He had no desire to make contact with anyone here except the livery owner.

As he approached the livery owner's door, he was met by the owner, who had a surprised look on his face.

"I didn't expect you to come back," the surprised man said.

"Well, I did. Is my mare ready?" Bass asked.

"Well, we got a slight problem," the livery owner said, glancing sideways.

"You mean, she is not fit?"

"Oh, the mare is much better, but I didn't think you would come back, so I promised to sell her to a local rancher."

"Why'd you do that? I paid you for her keep and care, and to my figurin', I's back before the time is up," Bass said.

"Well, you are, but this man wants her pretty bad, and I have promised him he could have her."

"All I can say is that I dealt with you fair and square, and I've killed one man for her already. I sure wouldn't wanta have to repeat that."

The livery man's mouth dropped open and his eyes widened as he took a step back and looked at Bass. He immediately knew that Bass was serious and that he had tried to play his hand on the wrong person.

"Wait, wait," the man said. "The mare is fine, and she is in the barn. There is no need to get excited. I only said that I had promised to sell her to the rancher if you did not come back. You've come back and, by the way I figure it, I owe you four dollars, which is the remainder of what you deposited. How does that sound?"

"Sounds like a right smart choice to me," Bass said.

"Mister, I did not mean to make you mad, and I hope you'll forgive me," the man said.

"You don't need to be forgiven for anythin' as you did nothin' wrong. You just misjudged a man. But I'd like to add that misjudgments can lead to some very unpleasant happenin's," Bass cautioned.

"I understand you totally. Let me get the money, and I will take you to the barn."

When he turned for the door, Bass added, "By the way, Miss Nancy said you owed her some money, and I should collect it while I'm here."

The man stood for a moment and thought.

"You know I think she is right. As I remember, I owe her ten dollars. Let me get that for you now."

"That would be good."

While the man was gone, Bass could not help but laugh. He had no idea that the man owed Miss Nancy money. He just wanted to make the man's day as uncomfortable as he had tried to make his.

The man returned with a ten dollar gold piece and anxiously placed it in Bass' hand.

"I hope there are no hard feelings, and that you give Miss Nancy my best," the man said.

"I'll be glad to," Bass said. "Now, let's get my mare."

The mare no longer had a limp. Her leg was still a little swollen, but the livery owner told Bass that it would probably always be that way. She still should make a fine brood mare, although she couldn't be expected to run again as she had before the injury.

The man had taken good care of the mare. It was obvious that he had had great plans for her if Bass had not returned. She was looking so well that it seemed even King was shaking his head in approval as Bass led her from the barn.

Bass stopped at the bank and deposited the ten dollars in Miss Nancy's account. The cashier seemed ill at ease, and even fumbled with the deposit slip while trying to look at Bass and write at the same time. As the clerk was doing this, it was apparent that all of the other employees were keeping a restless interest on this black man with two pistols hanging on his hips. They seemed to breathe a sigh of relief as he turned, tipped his hat and exited the door.

Bass' group stopped at the market and bought some bacon and hardtack. While they were there, Bass asked the clerk if he had seen the two men who had robbed and killed the owners of the general store. He replied no, but that he hoped that someday they would return, since the city had a rope ready for them. The town had suffered with the loss of a general store, the clerk said, and the town people vowed revenge for all the hardships these two men had caused.

Bass responded that if he had a chance someday, they might get their wish.

Bass, Mama and Jennie continued on their journey through Seminole Territory and into the Cherokee Nation. As they traveled, they passed sights that Bass had earlier filed into his memory, and some of them brought back thoughts of the past.

It was obvious that the women were getting tired of the journey, and when informed that one more day should be the end of their trip, they seemed to become more cheerful and slept better.

The next day, as the sun reached its highest, they topped the ridge and looked down on the Mankiller homestead. Bass sat in the saddle for a few moments while pointing out things on the farm that had happened since he had lived there. After this short visual tour, he let out the customary shout that startled the two ladies so much that their eyes had both looks of surprise and fear, while they tried to control their mounts.

Bass laughed and said, "Don't worry. This is the way you approach the house so that no one thinks trouble is on the way. You don't want to scare people here 'bouts or you might be facin' more problems than you wanta deal with."

While they descended the ridge and approached the creek, the door to the house swung open and, as usual, Little Sam and Sarah rushed onto the porch. This time, however, they just stood and watched as the three approached.

As the trio turned the corner of the corral, the children's excitement to see Bass overcame them. As usual, Little Sam led the foot race. As Sarah grew older, she had become a little shy, no longer exhibiting the fleetness of foot and lack of caution that she had in the past. This also was probably tempered with the fact that there were strangers with Bass. But when Bass got close enough, she could no longer control herself and hurried to get in line to share the greeting with Little Sam.

Another change was that Little Sam first extended his hand in a manly way, and then quickly lunged forward to grab Bass around the neck. This was the first time that Bass had realized how much of a change had taken place in the little boy he had first encountered when Sam and he had returned from the Battle of Pea Ridge.

As soon as there was room for her, Sarah rushed in, wrapping one arm around the other side of his neck. As if there were a magnet in it, her other hand shot to Bass' mustache and she began to tug on it while a smile broke across her face and her big brown eyes sparkled with delight.

Little Sam ran to get King's reins, as well as the tether on the mare and the packhorse. He looked up at the women and simply said, "Let's go to the house."

Sarah now had Bass' huge hand in hers and was leading him toward the porch. She was swinging their arms as they walked toward the house and had a skip in her gait. Sam and Lidia were standing with broad smiles on their face. They could no longer control themselves and rushed off the porch to greet their friend as if they had finally filled a missing place in their hearts.

Following the long and emotional greeting, Bass turned to introduce his mother and Jennie. They were welcomed warmly and told that they were now a part of the Mankiller family, and as such, they should come in and eat.

The meal was greatly appreciated, as trail food was far from the home cooking that Mama had fixed for so many years. Soon, it was time for bed. The trail had been long and hard, and all looked forward to peaceful sleep.

***

The next morning, Sam and Bass visited about what had taken place with English Bob. At the end of the tale, Sam said, "Good riddance. Did you scalp the bastard?"

"No, it never entered my mind. I don't think that there is much worry 'bout where he'll end up."

Sam then questioned Bass about how he had gotten his mother, and was shocked about the coincidence of running into Nancy.

Sam said, "Well, you have always said that things happen when they are supposed to happen, and my friend, it seems that you've continually been correct."

"Sam, I know we have just gotten here, but I have a real problem. I need to go after two fellers that I promised I'd take care of. I'm wonderin' if you'd mind lookin' after the ladies while I'm gone. I sure hate to ask you, but times wastin', and if I don't get on their trail, I might miss 'em."

"Bass, you know that whatever you need, Lidia and I are willin' to help. You go and do what you gotta do. We'll take care of your ladies for you."

Chapter 15

The Hunt

The sun was just breaking over the horizon when Bass finished packing his gear, along with the shotgun and pistol that he had taken from English Bob. Bass had decided that he might do two jobs at once. With his money in his pack, and the shotgun and pistol securely wrapped, he and King headed for Tahlequah.

He had two things on his mind. The most pressing was dealing with the men that Nancy had prepaid for him to deliver justice. His second thought was to possibly find a suitable place to move his family and start a new life.

When he got to Tahlequah the first thing he did was to ask where he might find Sam Sixkiller. Bass knew that if there was anyone who might know the whereabouts of these killers, it would be Sixkiller.

Ben Horsechief told Bass that Sam was on the trail to Van Buren to pick up supplies for the Light Horsemen, which explained why he was dragging a string of packhorses. Ben told Bass that Sam wanted him to come to Van Buren. The supplies that Sam was picking up were valuable, so he wanted another gun for the trip back. If Bass would wait for about two hours, Ben said he would join him.

Sam felt this was ideal since he had decided to take all of his funds from the bank and, while it did not greatly concern him, he sure would be much happier with another well-trained gun along on the trip.

Sam went to the bank, withdrew his funds and began his wait for Ben. The day was beautiful, and the moments of no activity were much appreciated. Bass realized that he had not had the privilege of just sitting and thinking in a long time.

He had heard that the port at Van Buren had caused the city to grow, and there were some farms for sale in the area. While he and Sam Mankiller had done well together, Bass felt the need to find a permanent home for his mother and to start his own horse operation. If the opportunity were right, he wanted to be ready to make his move, especially now that he had his freedom papers and there could not be anyone challenging his rights or freedom. There seemed to be nothing standing in his way.

King still was as good a stud as any and his production had proven to be far better than average. It seemed that King's blood mixed well with just about any mare, and his reputation for producing outstanding offspring had spread through the Nation. With Van Buren being about as active a place as there was for coming and going to the Nation, Bass was sure that a location there would be advantageous.

Ben was a pleasure to have as a companion on the journey. He was young, energetic and seemed to love the fact that he was doing a service for his people, especially since he was getting a decent living while doing something that he enjoyed.

Ben talked of all manner of things while they were on the road. Of course, he expressed his great admiration for Sam Sixkiller and the other Light Horsemen. He continually preached about how brave and honest Sam was and that he hoped, in some way, that he would be able to contribute to law and order the way Sam had.

Ben went on to say that he was only half Cherokee. His father had been white and killed in the conflict by those who had sought vengeance for the selling of the Cherokee land in the East. His father had not been directly involved in the conflict, only an unfortunate bystander in that bloody struggle. His mother had chosen her last name for him since he was going to be raised in the Cherokee lands and the only family that he would know would be hers.

"My Pa's family had a interesting past," Ben said. "Seems my grandpa was some kind of a mountain man who trapped fur in the Rockies and later hunted buffalo for the wagons that were traveling cross the country. He made his way down to New Mexico territory where he met my grandma. She was the daughter of a trader and muleskinner.

"My Pa was born and raised in New Mexico and left home at about fifteen. He started out as a muleskinner, traveled quite a bit and ended up scoutin' and leadin' wagon trains across the country.

"He met my Ma in New Mexico, where her family had set up a trading post south of Santa Fe. Her Pa had been a Cherokee scout for the army while they were chasin' the Apache. He later was sent to Texas, where he scouted against the Comanche.

"His greatest accomplishment was recruitin' the Tonkawa to help the army fight the Comanche. Seems like the Tonkawa were cannibals, and nobody liked 'em. In fact, most everybody feared 'em. That's why my Ma's Pa was so set on signin' 'em up. He knew the Comanche was scared to death of 'em because they feared if they was killed and eaten, they could not go to the happy huntin' grounds."

"You mean that the Tonkawa's ate people?" Bass asked.

"Yep, that's what cannibals do. They eat people and seem to take great delight in doin' it. When my Ma's Pa told the general about this, he said, 'I don't care how many Comanche they eat. In fact, I would hope they eat the whole damned tribe."

Bass said, "You know, that kinda makes my stomach turn. I been hungry in my life, but I never gave no thought of eatin' a person."

Ben lightly laughed. "My Ma says her Pa claimed that the Tonkawa was one of the reasons that there was finally some peace restored to the area.

"Anyhow, when he left the army, he used his musterin' out pay to buy a place in New Mexico with good water, and it turned into a really good business. He and my grandma were really doin' good, 'til some bastards decided that they didn't like seein' a Indian bein' successful and burned 'em out.

"That's when they all decided to move back to the Territory, including my Ma and Pa, who had married. They was doin' awright until my Pa got kilt."

Since his father's death, Ben said that Sam Sixkiller had become a great influence in his life. Sixkiller was Ben's mother's cousin. Sixkiller was often at family gatherings where he had shown Ben great kindness. Ben viewed him as the most important man in his life.

As they traveled, Ben said, "Now you know why I am a Light Horseman and proud to be able to ride in the same shadow as Sam. I only hope that I can be close to bein' as good as he is."

Bass said, "From what I know of Sam, you couldn't have picked a better man."

"I can tell you that Sam feels the same way about you. He often has told me stories about what an honorable and brave man you are. Bass, the stories he tells are told all over the Indian Nation and I feel there is not an honest Indian that wouldn't help you any way he could. Of course, there are a few that have bad ways — those shudder when they hear your name, but even those respect you. They know you will treat them fairly, and they honor men who have courage and a sense of rightness."

Bass said, "I swore that I would use my skills and time to do the right thing and the right way. My Mama always said, "Do the right thing even if no one else is doin' it. Just because everyone else is doin' the wrong thing don't make it right.

"I've always tried to do what is right, and I still feel that you got to treat all folks proper, even if you don't agree with what they're doin'."

As the day passed, they decided to spend the night at Godfrey's road-house. It would be a comfort not to sleep on the ground again, and it was a well-known fact that Godfrey's wife put on a good table for the guest. Road food sure could get old and boring, Bass and Ben agreed as they looked forward to a good night's sleep and comforting food.

While they put their horses in the barn, Ben noticed how carefully Bass carried the long blanket roll and his saddlebags.

"Bass, you got somethin' special there?"

"When we get to the room, I'll show you somethin' that I'll bet you never laid eyes on before."

Ben's eyes widened eager to see what this man, who had gained such a reputation, could have that would be such a surprise. Soon, his youth took over, and he started to act like a kid waiting for his Christmas package. He bounced up the stairs, quickly opened the door to their room and stood with a big grin on his face as he waited for Bass to close the door and place the bedroll on the bed.

"Well, let's see what you got," Ben urged.

Bass slowly unrolled the blanket. Even in the fading sunlight that splashed through the window, the elegance of the shotgun was undeniable. The silver of the barrels combined with the abundant gold inlay danced in the light.

Ben's mouth fell open as he stood staring.

"Can I touch it? Can I?" he eagerly asked.

"Sure."

Ben reached down, as if picking up a baby, and lifted the shotgun into his arms. He carried it with outstretched arms to the window where he could capture all of the sunlight possible. His eyes slowly traveled from one end of the weapon to the other, and then he slowly turned it over and repeated the inspection.

Returning the shotgun, Ben then picked up the pistol and gave it the same inspection. The pearl handle blended in with the silver excellently. The engraving on the pistol was, without a doubt, the work of a master.

When finished, Ben said, "You was sure right. I ain't seen anythin' like 'em in my life, and I doubt that I'll see anythin' like that again. Where'd you get 'em and what's you gonna do with 'em?

"You might say I got it as a prize for savin' my life, and I plan on turnin' 'em into somethin' useful for me and my family."

Ben said, "I's got no idea what's they're worth, but just by lookin', I'd say it would take a nobleman to own 'em."

"That's an interestin' thought, 'cause the feller that donated it to me claimed he was one. However, he died like an ordinary man, and according to my thinking, he died too fast."

They returned the shotgun to its protective blanket, before locking the room and going to eat. While enjoying the meal, Bass visited with Godfrey.

"Have two fellers about their mid-twenty's been by here of late? They woulda been ride'n a sorrel mare and a big paint horse. One of 'ems name is Avry and the other's name is Paul. Both of 'em woulda been loud talkin' and likin' their whiskey."

"My friend, you just described half of da customers we get, except for the paint horse and the names. A feller came through 'bout two days ago and said that he saw two no-goods chased out of a bar down in Eufaula, and one of 'em was ridin' a paint. He told me that I had better keep an eye out for 'em as they sure seemed to take no mind as to how they treated people.

"Seems they got in a fight in Fat Annie's place and got the hell kicked out of 'em. It probably would of ended up in a gunfight, but the two were in their drawers and not totin'.

"Anyways, they got throwed out in the street in their drawers, and it was only the goodness of Fat Annie's heart that she finally throwed their stuff out to 'em. Of course, she took ten dollars out of their pocket before she did it.

"These might be your men, but they ain't been by here, and I hope they don't show up."

"Well, if they do, I would appreciate it if'n you could get word to the Light Horse. I want 'em bad. They owe a debt, and I promised to see that they pay it."

"Bass, you have my word that if'n I see 'em or hear of 'em, I will get word to the Light Horse."

"Tell your wife how much we liked her fixin's, and if she ever wants to run you off, I have a place for her."

"She cooks good, but she sure does snore," the innkeeper said jokingly.

"Well, I don't know that a full belly would be a good trade for no sleep," Bass responded, continuing the jest.

All three men broke out in laughter and exchanged warm handshakes, before Bass and Ben headed for their room and a good night's sleep.

***

On arriving in Van Buren, Bass was impressed with the bustling streets, all the people going about their business. The port definitely had made this a much different place than to what he was accustomed. In the

Territory, most of the time, the local town was calm or even sleepy except on the weekend.

Bass paid special notice of how people looked at him and was relieved that his presence did not seem to attract any attention. Bass wondered if his being accompanied by Ben had anything to do with it, but he took it as a good sign. He also noticed several black men walking the street, and some working in stores. He took this as another sign that Van Buren might be the kind of place he was seeking.

As decided earlier, they met Sam at the sheriff's office, and while there, Sam introduced Bass to Sheriff Donavan.

"This is the best man I know when it comes to trackin' and fightin'," Sam said of Bass. "His word is solid, and you can count on him with your life."

The sheriff looked at Bass from head to foot, and then extended his hand.

"Anyone that Sam recommends like that is a friend of mine."

As they were exchanging handshakes, Bass said, "I'm lookin' for two guys named Avry and Paul. One is ride'n a paint horse. You seen 'em?"

"Sounds like you are looking for Avry Timken and Paul Younkers. I got a flyer on them the other day. They've been raising hell around Eufaula, and I was warned to be on the lookout for them."

"Sure fits what I've been told. You got any more word than that?" Bass asked.

"No, but these creatures don't usually change their habits. If I was lookin' for them, I'd head for Eufaula parts."

"Thanks, I really need these guys. While we're talkin', is there a good gun store here?"

"Yep, Joseph Minkenhas has a great shop and store two blocks down the street on the west side. You can't miss it. He's got everything you want, and he can fix anything that needs fixin'."

Sam said to Bass, "I know Mr. Joseph, done lots a business with 'im. I'll be glad to walk you down there and introduce you to 'im."

"Well, sheriff, I guess you're thinkin' you've met the question man, but I've got another. Do you think that I might be able to buy some land here bouts and settle my family down here?"

"With the introduction that Sam gave you, I'd be pleased to have you around. My brother died a while back, and his place is for sale. It's too big for his wife and kids to keep up, and it has some great potential. He never worked it like it should've been worked — spent too much time in the bar. It still made money. It's got a great creek bottom and some good land 'bout two miles out a town."

"You know what they want for it?"

"I think fifteen dollars an acre. It has one hundred and twenty acres. I know that is kind a high, but it has a nice house on it and a lot of potential. My brother was a good carpenter, when he was not drinkin'. A good man could really make something out of it," the sheriff assured.

"After I go to the gunsmith, could you take me out to look at it?"

"It'd be my pleasure," the lawman said.

"Then I'll be back in a while."

Sam, Ben and Bass led their horses down the street to the hitch in front of the gunsmiths shop. Bass took the blanket from King's pack, along with his saddlebags, and they all entered the store.

Joseph looked up from his workbench. "Sam, it's great to see you again. What can I do for you boys?"

"Joseph, this is Ben Horsechief and Bass Reeves."

"Nice to meet you boys. What can I do for you?" the friendly man asked.

Bass stepped forward and placed the blanket on the bench. He carefully unrolled it. When he had finished opening his parcel, Joseph stood up, but never took his eyes from the contents. He adjusted his glasses and stooped over for a better look.

Sam's mouth fell open as he whistled air.

Ben just stood there, smiling.

"My God, I have never seen anything like that shotgun. It must have come from Europe, from someone very wealthy. The pistol is outstanding as well. How did you come by these?" Joseph asked.

Bass stood for a moment and said, "Let's just say that the man that had 'em has no more use for 'em, and he was nice enough to donate 'em to me."

Joseph reached down and carefully picked the shotgun up. He turned it from side to side, slowly taking in its splendor.

After several moments of silence, he asked, "What do you have in mind?"

"I'd like to sell 'em." Bass said.

Joseph kept staring at the guns. He finally looked up, stroking his chin. He again adjusted his glasses and scratched his head while in deep thought.

"The shotgun is a work of art. I have never seen so much gold inlay, and the craftsmanship is unmatched. The ivory on the pistol and the engraving makes it very valuable as well.

"I can't pay you what they are worth, but if you will let me send it to the East, I know it will bring a fortune. I'll tell you what I will do. You can have anything in the store on credit, and when we get the sale, I will take twenty percent of what it brings. I have contacts in New York. In fact, my brother has a shop there. He has a lot of wealthy clients that seem to have more money than good sense. I know that one of them would love to add these exceptional pieces to their collection. I think they will bring eight hundred to a thousand dollars. What do you think of that deal?"

Now Bass was in shock. He stood and thought for a moment, then looked back at the shotgun and pistol. Now, he was the one stroking his chin.

"Well sir, looks like it is a tradin' day, you up to some heavy work?"

"Let's see where we go," replied Joseph, smiling.

Bass stepped toward the glass counter on the other side of the room and said, "To start with, I want to see one of those new Colts I've been hearin' about."

Before the morning was over, Bass had traded his Spencer and his two Remingtons for two new Colts and a Winchester rifle. The way he figured, after all was said and done, he had all of the newest and most trusted weapons possible, and when the sale in New York was done, he should receive at least six hundred dollars in cash.

Bass shared a lunch with Ben and Sam, and then said his goodbyes as they prepared to return to Tahlequah and he returned to the sheriff's office. The sheriff seemed eager to see him, and in a short time, they were headed to his sister's place.

The property was just as the sheriff had described. There was a great house. It was evident that the previous owner had been an exceptional carpenter. The house had three bedrooms and a long porch, from which there was almost a total view of the place.

The barn was not as outstanding, but Bass knew that he had the ability to make the additions of stalls and other improvements that would turn it into an appealing place to start his horse operation.

Bass walked the property, impressed with the number of acres just waiting to be turned into a productive commercial garden. He strolled up the hill back toward the house, calculating that the pastureland was great with just the right amount of shade for horses.

Returning to the house, he said, "Sheriff, let's head out. I have a lot of travelin' to do and need to get on down the trail."

As they were riding back to town, Bass said, "I like the place. Tell your sister that I will give her fifteen hundred dollars today for it."

"While you were walkin' the place, we visited, and she said that she would take seventeen hundred," the sheriff countered.

"If you can get her to take sixteen hundred, I will make a deposit of five hundred today and pay her the rest when I get back in about a week or two."

The sheriff took off his hat and wiped his forehead. "I'll tell you what I'll do. I have been admirin' that stallion of yours ever since you came to town, and if you let me breed my mare to him, the deal is done."

"Great, let's get to town and meet with the lawyer."

The meeting was short, and the papers were drawn. The attorney gave Bass a paper and told him to take it to the bank. He was to give the banker the paper and the five hundred dollars. Everything would be finalized when Bass returned in two weeks.

At the bank, Bass got the usual reception. His color and the fact that he was carrying two guns seemed to make people with money uneasy. But when he showed the clerk the paper from the attorney, the atmosphere changed. It really changed after he took his saddlebag to the clerk and made his deposit.

Bass stayed in town that night and hit the trail early the next morning. He put King to the test, making good time towards Eufaula. This was a new route for him, and he was noting all of the landmarks he could. As always he continually stored this kind of information for further reference.

About noon, he heard the sound of a shotgun blast, followed by the report of a pistol. Noticing that the sounds came from the other side of the ridge, he could not help but investigate.

On topping the ridge, he put his head close to King's neck as he entered a thicket of trees. In the bottom below, he could see a small cabin while hearing loud shouting. However, Bass wasn't close enough to understand what was being said.

He dismounted, tied King to a tree, withdrew his new Winchester and slowly worked his way down the hill. When about a hundred yards from the cabin, he found a location where he could rest his Winchester on a rock while having full view of the happenings below.

Bass watched as Avry stepped from a small grove of trees, pushing a man in front of him, while holding onto the man's suspenders. Avry had his pistol pointed at the back of the man's head as the duo slowly started walking toward the house.

"Girly, why don't you throw out that scatter gun and come on out here? All we wants to do is play with you!" Avry asked of someone in the house.

There was a reply from the house, but it was so weak that Bass could not tell what was being said.

"Now, girly, we has wasted 'bout as much time as we is gonna. If you don't throw out that gun and come on out here, we is gonna have to shoot your Pa. Then I promise that our dealin' with you will be less fun," Avry threatened.

The door on the cabin opened, and a girl of about fifteen stepped onto the porch. She still had the shotgun in hand, but it was at her side.

"Please don't hurt my Pa. My Ma just died last month, and he's all I got left. But I is scared of you."

"Well, this is you last chance. Throw that gun down and come here, or I'll kill him!" Avry growled, pulling back the gun's hammer while placing the barrel closer to the farmer's head.

Bass knew that he had waited as long as he could. He sighted his rifle and pulled the trigger.

Avry's hat immediately left his head as he automatically grabbed his exposed head and turned toward where the shot had come from. A puzzled look crossed the outlaw's face.

"Avry," Bass shouted. "That was just to get your attention. I've got one ready for your head."

The sound of his name caused Avry caused him to lose his focus on the man in front of him and he began trying to figure from where the shot and voice came. Refocusing, he turned to locate the man who was now at his feet in a fetal position. Avry started to point his pistol back toward his victim.

Bass fired again, this time shooting the pistol from Avry's hand.

"I told you I had one ready for you, and this time I am gonna put it in your eye. Now, tell Paul to come on out of that thicket, or I'll sure end your miserable life here and now."

Avry was shaking his stinging hand, nearly dancing with the pain. However, he quickly realized that he was as close to death as he cared to be and composed himself.

"Paul, get out here now!"

"I ain't comin' out," a voice in the thicket said.

"If you don't come out, this bastard's gonna kill me! Get your ass out here!" Avry shouted.

Bass now shouted. "Paul, I got you in my sights, and I would just as soon plug you now as wait. Throw your gun out and come on out, or I'll help you lead the way to hell for Avry!"

With that, Paul threw out his pistol and exited the thicket, straining his eyes to locate the source of this voice that he thought he recognized.

"Now, both of you drop to the ground and spread your arms away from your body. Mister, I want you to take that scatter gun and cover 'em while I come on down."

The man, who had hurried to his daughter's side, released her from his embrace and with a look of pleasure, grabbed her shotgun and placed it to his shoulder.

In a short time, Bass had led King down the side of the hill and secured the men's hands behind them.

When finished, he asked them, "Boys, do you recognize me now? You know I've had you in my sights three times. I am now convinced that the worst thing I've done wasn't to finish you the first time. However, don't worry. I am takin' you to Atoka. I understand that the good folks there have a hankerin' to talk to you."

***

A crowd started to gather when Bass rode into Atoka, pulling the two men behind him. They were not accustomed to seeing a black man, especially a black man escorting two white men. Slowly, the town people began to recognize the two men as the pair that had killed the general store owner and his partner, then burned the building to the ground. All of the parts were coming together as Bass reached the sheriff's office — the black man was the one with the widow Nancy when she came to town to bury her husband and uncle. Now the black man had brought the bastards back to stand trial.

Bass pushed the two men into the sheriff's office, just at the sheriff was starting toward the door. Bass simply said, "Here are Avry and Paul. They killed Miss Nancy's husband and uncle. I hear you want to give 'em a fair trial, and then hang 'em. I've done my job. It's up to the good people to do theirs.

"Now, if you will do two things for me, I will be movin' on. First, check the wanted posters and see if there is any money on the two."

The sheriff was speechless, but stumbled toward his desk. He went through a stack of papers in his drawer, finally pulling out two flyers.

"Looks like there is a total of three hundred dollars on these bastards," the sheriff said.

"I figured there was someone wanted 'em pretty bad. Might you have it sent to Sheriff Donavon's office in Van Buren? I'll pick it up there, if that's alright with you. I don't wanta have to come back here to get it.

"Then, might you send a telegraph to Miss Nancy in Paris, Texas. Tell 'er that the men are here, and that Bass Reeves brought 'em in. It might help you get your store back if she is pleased with the outcome of the trial."

The sheriff, still in a daze said, "Yes, sir."

Bass nodded back turned and exited the sheriff's office. After mounting King, Bass tipped his hat to the still gathering crowd and slowly started his return trip to home.

***

As he rode, Bass thought back over the past few days. The thing that most stood out in his mind was that a white man had called him sir. While the gun was an awful thing in the wrong hands, it sure seemed to change some attitudes in the right ones'.

Chapter 16

The Homestead

As he rode back to Sam's place, Bass' thoughts turned to all the great things that had happened with him and the Mankillers. Surely, he could never again in his life find people so kind and supportive. Nonetheless, he knew that it was time for him to move to a new life with new prospects for developing the kind of freedom that he had always craved.

Parting with the Mankillers would be hard, but he knew that he would return from time to time to continue his relationship with the family. He especially was going to miss watching the children grow up. They had changed so much since he first arrived. It was hard to imagine how much more they would change in his absence.

After he arrived and settled in, Sam and Bass had a long talk about what Bass now wanted to do with his life. Sam totally understood what was driving Bass. He and Lidia both agreed that Bass needed a new start after all that had happened. With Mama and Jennie now with him, making a change would come more easily.

"You know, I have been thinkin'," Sam said. "You and King have carried a big part of the burden on developin' this place, and I've decided that the only fair thing is for you to take the gray mare and Blaze, as well as the Englishman's mare. As a matter of fact, you can take all the horses, except I would like to keep one of the fillies, now that she is bred to King. Hopefully, she produces a great foal. I will leave it to you which one I keep. This should give you a great start on your horse operation. I feel that I don't deserve anymore from you. Your dedication to my family and the fact that you saved them will never be forgotten.

"You have helped build this place into a home that I probably would never had, so go with my best wishes. Just promise me that you'll return from time to time. You'll be greatly missed here," Sam said.

Later, Bass had a more painful talk with the children. Both of the children hated to see him go and expressed their love and respect for the man who had come to be such an important part of their lives. They insisted that he return often, warning him that if he did not come back, they would come looking for him.

The day of their departure was a somber affair. The sadness, however, was broken when Little Sam announced that he was going to change his name.

"Why you want to do that?" Bass asked.

"Well, I think I need to start lookin' for a girl, and I am afraid that my name might scare them off," Little Sam speculated.

"Well, Mankiller may not be the most appealin' name, but it is one filled with honor," Bass noted.

"I know, that's why I have decided to change my name to Francis Mankiller," Little Sam said.

There was a moment of silence, and then huge laughter erupted from everyone. None of them laughed more than Little Sam.

"Well, I got you on that one, Bass," Little Sam said.

***

When Bass got to Van Buren, he first went to the sheriff's office where he was pleased to find the reward for the two outlaws was waiting. Giving Sheriff Donavan the money, Bass promised that as soon as he could get to the bank, he would pay the balance for the land.

"You know," the sheriff said, "The place is vacant now, and if you want, you can start movin' in."

Better words could not be found, as Bass realized they meant he had a place to take his Mama and Jennie right away.

***

Mama could hardly believe her son had bought a home for them, much less one that far exceeded her dreams. Nonetheless, she immediately set to work as if she were sixteen again. Her excitement made all of her movements look like she was dancing. Plus, she put Jennie to work, which wasn't hard since the younger woman's enthusiasm was as great as Mama's.

"You two put me to shame," Bass said. "You all has spit and shined this place until it looks like a new dollar. I feel like I've shirked my duties. All I've done is started the new barn. I just can't seem to match you ladies."

While the ladies were changing the house, Bass stayed busy working on the barn and corral. He made up his mind that if he was going to produce fine horses, he had to have a fine place to show them off.

However, he soon realized that he needed more than his own hands to accomplish what he wanted done. So, Bass went to town to see if he could hire some men to help. This turned into a bigger challenge than he had anticipated.

The man at the saw mill was happy to take his money, but when Bass asked if he knew some men wanting to work, he looked at him like he had asked if he could eat dinner with him.

"Mister, I doesn't think you can hire anyone in this here town," the man said.

"Why is that? My money is good," Bass said.

"It ain't your money that will hold you back," the man said. "There just ain't no people here 'bouts that would take kindly to havin' a man your color for a boss."

Bass thought for a moment, and then asked, "Well, where do the people 'my color' live in this town?"

Bass followed the man's directions and found a small grocery store, where he inquired about help. The storekeeper looked puzzled for a moment. He couldn't remember the last time a Negro had come in and said he wanted to hire someone.

On the storekeeper's recommendation, Bass went to a small shack and asked if the boys were there. In a few minutes, he was greeted, hesitantly, by Pete and Joseph. They had a look of suspicion on their faces when Bass started to talk, but the more he talked, the more relaxed they became.

Grins then filled their faces when he told them that if they worked out, he would need them to work for several months.

"Mr. Bass, our mama is sick, and we can't afford to buy enough food for the other kids, much less buy her medicine," Pete said.

"I'll tell you what I'll do," Bass said. "I'll pay you fifteen dollars a month each, and feed and house you. I'll give you fifteen dollars now, so you can leave food for the others and get your ma's medicine, and I'll let you use a horse for one of you to come back here every night."

"Mr. Bass that sounds like the answer to our prayers, but would it be possible for both of us to comes in on Sunday? We would like to take Mama and the kids to church," Joseph asked.

"Boys that would please me to no end. We have a deal."

***

The three men worked diligently and a strong friendship developed between them. Pete and Joseph were hard workers and learned rapidly. Before long, the old barn was converted to a stable with eight stalls, and the corral was constructed with a round pen for breaking horses and a large loafing area for the horses in the daytime.

When the stable was finished, Bass put his two new workers in the garden area. Before long, the three of them had an area of more than ten acres cleared and turned. It was starting to look like the place that Bass had envisioned.

The days turned into months. There seemed to be no end to what Bass could conjure up, and if there was a lull, it was sure that Mama had things she wanted done at the house.

One day, as they were working outside, two horsemen rode up. They both were well armed and sat in the saddle as if they were born there. They leaned forward in their saddles and looked the three men over.

One of them asked, "Which one of you is Bass Reeves?"

Bass looked the man in the eye and said, "I am." He then stared at the two for a minute before returning the question, "Who are you?"

"I'm Lenny Mann, and this is my brother, Lester.

"We are in need of your help. Seems that two outlaws have fled to the Territory and when we went in, no one would talk to us. It seems they have blended into the ground. I want them bad, and I am willing to pay you three dollars a day to lead us and find 'em. If we find 'em, there is a three hundred dollar reward for 'em, and I'd give you one hundred on top of the pay," Lenny concluded.

Bass looked up from his work and pushed his big brimmed hat back on his head. Then he wiped his forehead. He stood for a moment and looked more closely at the men.

"I'm wonderin' who sent you?" he finally asked.

"Sheriff Donavan said that if there was anyone in these parts that could snake these critters out, it would be you," Lenny said.

"How long have they been gone?"

"We been lookin' for them for a week now," Lester said.

"Right smart lead they got. Tell you what I'd do. I'll go with you, but it'll cost you four dollars a day, and if'n we catch 'em, I get half the reward," Bass negotiated.

"That is a pretty big bite you want," Lester protested.

"You said you wanted 'em, and now I'm seein' how bad you want 'em. Tell you what I'll do. If we don't get 'em, you pay me two dollars a day. But if we get 'em, I get the four dollars a day and all of the reward. I got a feelin' you want these two for personal reasons, not for the law," Bass said.

The two men turned their horses and road several yards away from where the negotiations had been taking place. Stopping, they talked for a moment, and then returned.

"Here's the offer. If we catch them in one week, the deal is as you stated, but if it takes more than a week, you get three dollars a day and half the reward," Lenny said.

Bass thought a few moments before asking, "Where do you think they entered the Territory?"

"We think they were headed toward Tahlequah," Lester said.

"Then you got a deal," Bass said, hearing the right word, Tahlequah. "I'll meet you at the sheriff's office at eight in the mornin'. My time starts then."

"Done. At eight it is," Lester said.

After the men left, Bass asked his hired hands if one of them would stay in the barn, even on Sunday, while he was gone. Bass offered an extra five dollars for the Sunday work. He knew Mama and Jennie could handle the chores while he was away, but he did not want to leave them alone on the property. The brothers had already proven themselves, so he had no fear of problems, he was glad when they agreed to his proposal.

***

The next morning, the trip started as planned, except Bass was pushing the group at a faster pace than they had expected. As they rode, they talked. The two men were both lawmen from the Kansas area, but they had a personal interest in finding their two outlaws. Their brother had also been a lawman in Kansas, until these two men shot him in the back while he was on his rounds. Now, the two brothers wanted to make sure the culprits paid for their cowardly deeds.

As they talked, it became clear to Bass that they were tough men. They had both, along with their brother, been buffalo hunters and worked in the west Texas area. They were involved in several conflicts with the Comanche. The mere fact that they were alive today was proof that they were skilled survivors.

The trail was cold, but Bass knew that if he could make contact with members of the Cherokee, he could get a lead on their whereabouts. His plan soon came about. Fortunately, the first person he came upon was his old friend from Tahlequah, Ben Horsechief. Ben had been in pursuit of a whiskey runner for the past several days and had covered most of the area where Bass expected the two culprits to be hiding.

Bass' luck was with him. Ben said he saw two guys that fit their description at a camp about two miles to the west just the day before.

Knowing the area well, Bass pushed the group with all haste. In less than thirty minutes they were at the abandoned site.

Bass dismounted and studied the ground. He returned to the horses and said, "I got 'em. They're 'bout two hours ahead of us. Let's ride. I think they're headed for Tahlequah, but let's see."

Lester and Lenny were amazed at how easily Bass seemed to read the trail. They were covering the ground at a fast trot and, from time to time, Bass would point out a sign that assured them they were on the right trail.

Bass knew the trail, and he knew that there was a cabin in the next hollow that often was used for rest stops. The people there often sold whiskey to those who were seeking shelter or refreshments, and he also had heard that there was a woman there who provided other comforts to strangers.

As they topped the ridge, Bass held out his hand and said, "Best we stop here for a while. I think that we will be rewarded in a few minutes."

After a period of watching and not seeing anything unusual, Bass said, "I'm goin' down to the cabin and take a look. If I come out and head on down the trail, it means they're there. If I signal for you to come on down, then we need to get back on the trail."

The men nodded, and Bass headed for the cabin.

Once at the house, Bass dismounted, slowly walked toward the porch and looked into the open door. Seeing a woman inside, he talked to her for a few moments, and then tipped his hat, returned to King and mounted. Leaving, he put King into a gentle walk toward Tahlequah. As he reached the top of the trail, he turned to see what events would transpire.

Before Lester and Lenny could mount, the two men they were seeking came out on the porch. They were laughing, showing every sign that they had partaken of all the hospitality that the house offered. They stumbled toward their horses.

While the outlaws stumbled clear of the house, both lawmen pulled their rifles from their boots and took position. The years of buffalo hunting had prepared the men for this moment.

Within moments, two loud roars came from the men's Sharps and shattered the stillness of the morning. Both men fell, grasping their legs as they crashed to the ground. They each tried to gain their footing, but the pain and the accuracy of the bullets made their escape impossible.

As they lay cussing and grasping their shattered legs, Lester and Lenny began their approach with their buffalo rifles trained on the two men twisting on the ground.

The Mann brothers sat on their mounts as they took turns calmly talking in low voices to their prey. When they finished, Lenny covered the two struggling men with his pistol while Lester threw his lariat over both men. The rope settled around their waist and pulled their arms tight against their bodies. Lester then slowly backed his horse until the lariat was tight, securely pulling their bodies together.

Bass, still watching from a distance, then saw Lenny ride up next to the men and again speak. He looked as calm as someone going to a church social.

The two outlaws started to struggle, and their voices soon were distinguishable in the morning air as they began begging for mercy. Then they began shouting at the top of their lungs.

Lester simply turned and whipped his horse.

The sudden jerk of the rope pulled both men onto their faces; their legs were flailing as their bodies tumbled over the rocky ground. Lester kept his horse at a full gallop for several minutes. The outlaws' bodies grew limp as Lester continued to spur his horse and drag them again across the ragged rocks that jutted up from the ground around the cabin.

Bass silently watched the execution of the two. He could not help but think that this was about as bad a way to die as he had ever witnessed. He knew that the men deserved to be eliminated, but was glad that he had not been a part of it.

Lester stopped his horse, which was now somewhat struggling with the combined weight of the two pulverized bodies.

The Mann brothers walked to the corpses and looked at them for some time. As Bass approached, they turned and looked at him for a mo- ment before Lester said, "They made their bed. Now they have to sleep in it. We will take the bodies to Van Buren for identification and instruct the sheriff to pay you the bounty."

Lester reached in his pocket and handed Bass a ten-dollar coin. "You earned every penny of it. I'll pass the word that if anyone needs a tracker, that you're the man. Now, you may as well get on the road home. We are finished here. Thank you for your help."

Bass tipped his hat and said, "You fellers have a good trip. It has been a real eye-opener workin' with you."

"Well. if you think we was too brutal, remember that they shot our brother in the back, and he will never walk again," Lester said.

Bass turned King and started towards Tahlequah. Since he had told Mama and Jennie that he would probably be gone a week, he decided he might as well go over to the Mankilllers' place and see what was happening there. It had been too long since he had seen them, and while he was truly excited about the improvements he had made at his new place, he also felt some shame in not having taken time to visit his friends.

Chapter 17

The Return

When he topped the ridge and looked down on the valley that had been such an important part of his life, Bass could not help but feel like he was home again.

In his excitement, he nearly forgot to let out the greeting that was expected. When he finally did, he was relieved to see the front door open and Lidia step onto the porch. She strained her eyes toward he ridge while pushing the sleeves up on her dress.

Finally, she recognized him and hurried down the steps. She was nearly at full speed when Bass turned the corner of the corral. She stopped and straightened her apron and pushed her hair into place.

Bass pulled King to a halt, dismounted and rushed toward her. She jumped into his arms, grabbing him around the neck.

After this cheerful greeting, he placed her on the ground, and more normal conversation began.

"It has been too long since you were here. We have missed you so much and have often wondered how you're doing," Lidia said.

"You don't know how much I have thought of you all. I was in the Territory, and I just had to stop and visit for a while. How's everybody?"

"They're all fine. Sarah is in boarding school and won't be back for two more months. We sure miss her here, but she needed more schooling than I had time for. She wrote us a letter and said she was fine and loving all the learning she is getting.

"Sam and Little Sam are in town getting some supplies. They should be back in an hour or two. Come in the house and have some coffee. We can visit, and you can tell me all about your new place and Mama and Jennie."

***

In about two hours, Bass and Lidia heard the sound of horses in full gallop. The horses pulled to a full stop and in seconds the two Sams were rushing through the door.

"We saw King tied to the corral and came running," Sam said. "We're so glad to see you. How are you, and how is everyone back home? And what are you doing, and how is the new place?"

"Hold up!" Bass said. "You're not any happier to see me than I am you all, but you need to ask me one question at a time."

Sam grasped Bass' hand and wrapped his arm around his neck while Little Sam had his other hand and was smiling like he had a big secret. As soon as Bass released Sam's hand, Bass reached out and pulled Little Sam to him.

"You sure have grown. Oh my word, you're growing so. You're gonna be a big man."

As the excitement subdued, all were able to visit and share the stories of what had taken place since Bass left.

The most exciting bit of information, however, was that Bass had married Jennie, and she was going to have a child in the near future. The news was greeted with great joy and laughter. It was evident that both families were doing well, and time was being good to all the members of the families.

Bass departed the next morning. Returning to his old home and family had filled him with joy. He hated that he had not seen Sarah, but promised to return when she was back from school.

As he rode, he welcomed the warmth of the sun shining on his face, the feel of the open country and the beauty of the hills. He knew this land like the back of his hand, so he could relax in the saddle and let King work his way back home.

The calm of the morning, however, was shattered by the sound of gunfire in the distance. At first he heard only a few shots, but as he got closer, the gunfire turned into a full-scale battle.

Bass quickly headed King toward a ridge above the area where he thought the gunfire sounds were coming. From the top of the ridge, he could see three men on the high ground raining rifle fire down on about six men in the valley below.

Bass sat and watched, finally determining that the men in the valley were members of the Light Horse. He was sure of that when he recognized Ben Horsechief trying to work his way up the hill. Horsechief was making a brave effort, but the blistering fire kept pushing him to the ground.

Bass concluded that the three in the advantage position were wanted for something and did not plan to give themselves up to the law. He had no idea why the three were wanted, but knew that his friends were in a fix. The high ground gave the trio a tremendous advantage, and while they were using it well, fortunately they had not hit any of the Light Horsemen.

Nonetheless, Bass knew the situation could change at any minute, and he recognized it was his responsibility to help his friends.

So, Bass pulled his Winchester from the boot and took a position where he was resting his rifle on the top of a rock. He judged the distance to be about two hundred yards and adjusted his aim accordingly. Just before he pulled the trigger, he was sure he recognized one of the cornered men. It was Willy Davis, a freedman who had been nothing but trouble in the Territory for years. Willy had never been violent, but he was always on the edge of some kind of troubling activity, from whiskey running to horse thieving. Now, however, it appeared his endeavors were more than just small time activities.

Bass thought for a moment. He did not want to kill someone, but he sure did not want any of his friends to get hurt. Since Willy knew him, Bass wondered if he could convince Willy to give up, especially when Willy learned that it was surrender or find himself in the sites of a great marksman.

Bass took a deep breath, settled into a resting position and slowly squeezed the trigger. As quickly as he had fired, he chambered another round and pulled the trigger again. He then observed his work.

Both Willy's and one of his companion's hats were gone, and the men were scrambling to locate the source of the shots. While the men fought panic, Bass shouted down, "Boys, this is Bass Reeves, and I don't want to hurt you, but you better stop your shootin' and start doin' some thinkin'. If I wanted, both of you woulda been dead. So, throw your guns over the edge and put your hands where I can see 'em."

Willy was still crouched, but his hand was feeling where his hat had been. He started to talk to the other two in the rock fortress.

Bass had his rifle aimed and was waiting for a response from the three. No response came, but he could tell that they were still talking.

All of a sudden, the one with the remaining hat raised his rifle and fired before turning and making a run toward their horses. Bass calmly squeezed his trigger, and the fleeing man fell, grabbing his leg. In the same instant, the other two hoisted their rifles above their heads and began shouting, "Don't shoot! Don't shoot! We gives up!"

"Smart move," Bass assured the men. "Now, throw your rifles and your side arms down the hill. And don't do nothin' stupid. You're nearly safe and alive. Don't change that."

Bass then shouted to the Light Horsemen that he had the trio covered, so his friends could come and get them. "Be careful," Bass warned. "I can't tell if the downed man has a gun or not."

The man on the ground proved to be no problem since he was nursing his leg and had figured out that he was Bass' anytime Bass wanted to take him out.

After the arrest, Bass made his way down the mountain. He was delighted to see several Light Horsemen that he knew, including Ben Horsechief.

Ben said, "You really pulled us out of a hole. We just couldn't get a bead on 'em, and they sure were makin' us scratch dirt. I was tryin' to get up the hill for a shot, but there was just too much fire. If'n you hadn't come along, it woulda been a long day. What in the world were you doin' here anyway?"

"I've been visitin' the Mankillers and heard the commotion. I kinda figured you guys could use some help when I saw what was happenin'. So, I just joined in," Bass explained.

"Well, we sure do thank you."

"What were Willy and the boys up to any how?" Bass asked.

"It's a funny thing," Ben said. "If he hadn't joined with these Indian fellers, he could have gone free. But, since he did, we're gonna arrest him along with the others for robbin' the Middleman's Store and wingin' Mr. Middleman."

"I'm just glad no one got hurt, and that I could help you fellers," Bass said. "I know you have a hard job, and anytime I can help I will."

"Well, it was really appreciated. Anything we can do for you, just ask" Ben said.

Bass tipped his hat and exchanged handshakes with the other Light Horsemen. Before mounting King, he stopped, turned and said, "Say Ben, next time you get a chance, come by my place over by Van Buren. I think we should have a little talk. I kind a like the way you handle things, and I might have somethin' for you."

Chapter 18

Years Go By

Over the next few years, the farm exceeded Bass' plans. The vegetable production expanded to more than twenty acres, and his horses became known throughout the county. The farm was not the only thing that was productive. Jennie and Bass continued to have children, and they each took their place in the overall operation of the enterprise.

Pete and Joseph became a permanent part of the farm, a blessing for the Reeves' operation because Bass was regularly called upon to lead lawmen into the Territory. Bass loved the farm, but the tracking assignments were much more profitable. His absences made Pete and Joseph invaluable to the Bass home.

Bass' choice of Van Buren as his hometown was enhanced by the fact that the U.S. Marshal's office was located in Van Buren. Marshal Upton and Bass became an unbeatable team, meaning that they generally got anyone they pursued.

One cold and bitter day, Marshal Upton sent for Bass. The deputy arrived with instructions for Bass to prepare for a long and hard journey. The marshal's office had news that four men who had robbed a bank in Missouri now were holding up in the Territory. The deputy told Bass that the men were extremely dangerous; they had avoided or shot their way out of all attempts to capture them. In fact, they had killed two deputies just the week before, and Marshal Upton vowed that these outlaws would pay for those men's lives if he had anything to do with it.

Bass saddled Blaze and checked his supplies. He told Jennie and Mama that he would be gone awhile. He kissed all the kids and instructed them to behave. It was the usual parting with Pete and Joseph as they knew what to do as well as Bass. Like always, they would keep the operation going in his absence.

"Well Marshal, it sounds like we've got a real challenge facin' us," Bass said upon arriving at Marshal Upton's office.

"Bass, these guys are as bad a bunch as we've ever gone up against. They took over nine thousand dollars from the bank in Missouri and killed a clerk while doin' it. Then they ambushed the citizens that was trailing them and killed two more. Deputy Clarkson and Mathews had them cornered in the Territory, and both got wounded in the process. While they were lyin' helpless, the bastards simply walked up and murdered 'em. I want these guys as bad as any I've ever gone after."

"Sounds like we've got our work cut out for us. Who's goin' with us?" Bass asked.

"It's goin' to be the two of us and four deputies. I've been authorized to pick up any help that I might need in the Territory. The bank in Missouri has sent us five-hundred dollars to pay for anything that we might need in the hunt. I have budgeted two hundred of that for you, and if these guys are who I think they are, there should be reward money for them, and you'll sure get your share of that. My only hope is that we collect it."

"Well, Marshal, we hardly ever fail, and sounds like we'd better not this time."

***

The trip was miserable. The cold north winds were piercing, and the accompanying drizzle made every inch of the journey a test of the group's toughness. But the weather had to take a back seat, the men they were after were to great a threat to be ignored.

In their journey, the marshal told Bass that from now on he would be working out of Fort Smith. They had moved the court and the main marshal's station there. Marshal Upton explained that it would make no difference in their relationship. He promised that anytime he needed an accomplished tracker, Bass would be it.

As they continued on in the cold, Bass finally said, "Marshal, I think these guys ain't 'bout to be out and about in this weather. They've got to be holed up in some house or town. Where did Clarkson and Mathews get it?"

"Just a little north of Wagner," the marshal said.

"Then, let's go to Wagner and see if'n I can pick up their trail from there."

On the way to Wagner, the six of them stopped at a roadhouse. Bass warmed himself for about thirty minutes, and then left the group so he could visit a friend who lived in the area.

Tom Knifechief had no idea why anyone would be out in such weather, so he was doubly surprised to see his friend Bass, who didn't even live nearby.

"Tom, I need your help," Bass said.

"I didn't figure you came out on a night like this just to be sociable," Tom said. "I'm guessin' it's 'bout 'em two deputies that got kilt."

"You know I'd like for it to be social, but you're right. I came to see if'n you know anythin'."

"I heard it was a terrible killin'. Them deputies put up a hell of a fight, and then to get slaughtered like helpless pigs. I was talkin' to my friend Russell. He saw it happen, and he said them no-goods just seemed to think it was some kind of fun. And when they finished their dirty work, they headed down toward Wagner. If'n I was a bettin' man, I'd guess they is holed up in one of them drinkin' and girly houses there."

"Sounds like a good bet to me," Bass said. "Did you get any kind of description of these fellers?"

"All I know is they is bad, but they was ridin' a sorrel, a black and two grays. One of 'em has a bad arm. I don't know which one, but Russell said he was carrin' it like he had been hit," Tom said.

"Sounds like he maybe needs a doc. Is there a doc in Wagoner?"

"I thinks there is two, but I don't know for sure. They don't treat Indians," Tom said.

"I figure that's a good place to start lookin'," Bass said. "I thank you for your help, Tom, and now I need to get back on the trail."

As they stepped on the porch, Tom asked, "Where's King? I never thought I'd see you without 'im."

"He's served me well, and now, most of the time, all I want him to do is eat and make babies. This is Blaze. He is one fine critter, and I think he's maybe as good as King. Time will tell, but up to now, he has sure proven he can do the job."

"Well, good luck my friend, and if'n I can help you again, stop by. We've got to get rid of all these no-goods we can. This place just seems like it's drawin' more mavericks than we can stand," Tom said.

Bass nodded his head and quickly mounted. The cold kept him from exchanging any more conversation.

***

Bass told Marshal Upton what he learned, and the two decided that they should move with all speed at first light to Wagoner. Hopefully, they could catch their prey unprepared, and, if luck prevailed, they would be hung over and less of a threat.

The lawmen departed before daylight and were blessed with the strange weather that made the Territory famous. The sun broke through the clouds, and after a few more miles, the day turned pleasant and even comfortable.

Better weather allowed the group to move with more speed. By early afternoon, they were in Wagoner.

Marshal Upton sent one of the deputies to find the doctors to learn if one of them might know of a wounded stranger in town. In the meantime, two other deputies began asking their contacts for any information on strangers in town for the last few days.

Bass went to the livery stable and looked for the horses Tom had described. He was pleased to find a match.

The men all met back at the café and exchanged information. One of the doctors had treated a man with a minor gunshot wound to his shoulder. The wounded man had paid with a bank note from a Missouri bank. The doctor said the wound was not bad, but he had told him to come back that afternoon to get the dressing changed. He remembered, too, that the injured man said he was staying at Katie's Place.

The group decided they would wait and hope the wounded man returned to the doctor's place. That way, they could take him by surprise. Taking out one of the killers would improve the group's odds and, hopefully, make it easier to bring in the others.

Marshal Upton said, "Bass, you go down and get by the doc's office. When our boy gets there, take 'im out. I don't care how you take 'im, just make sure he don't come back to Katie's Place."

Bass left immediately. He quickly found a place where he could sit and wait, in front of the store across the street from the doctor's office. He pulled his hat down over his eyes and assumed the position of a person taking a nap in the much-appreciated sunshine.

In less than an hour, Bass observed a man coming down the street with his arm in a sling. Bass waited until the man was about to enter the doctor's office before he pulled his Winchester from behind his back and leveled it at the man.

"If'n I were you, I'd stand real still and not reach for your gun, 'cause if'n you do, I'll be glad to end your miserable life," Bass said in a voice that commanded attention.

The man froze for a moment, and then turned toward the voice. He found himself staring down the barrel of Bass' rifle and the urge to reach for his pistol faded rapidly.

"Now, with your fingers, pull your pistol and throw it on the ground," Bass continued. "Before, you do that, I want you to know that Deputy Mathews was a friend of mine, and I sure would like a reason to help you join him."

The man stalled for a moment. He seemed to be assessing all of his possibilities, but realized that he had no chance of beating the slug aimed at his heart.

He dropped his gun as instructed, and Bass crossed the street and roughly manacled his hands behind him.

"You made a wise move. We'll let the judge decide your fate," Bass said solemnly.

Bass took the man directly to the sheriff's office and had him placed in jail. He then hurried back to the café to report his success.

Marshal Upton was pleased, saying, "Now, we have to get them others at Katie's. How do you think we should do that?"

One of the deputies volunteered, "Me and Taylor will work our way around to the back of the buildin' to cut off their escape, so the rest of you can take 'em from the front. Their horses are in the livery, so they shouldn't be able to get far, even if they can get out the front."

"Ok, let's try that," Marshal Upton agreed. "But who is goin' in to get 'em?"

Bass said, "I'll go in. I'm the one that's less likely to cause attention."

Marshal Upton and the two deputies worked their way down the street, and then took positions opposite the front of Katie's place. Meanwhile, Bass calmly walked down the street before turning to enter the establishment.

Just as he was about to enter the front door, he heard the unmistakable crack of a Winchester from the upstairs window. He turned in time to see one of the deputies on the other side of the street stand, and then slump over the water trough in front of him. A barrage of fire from the upstairs windows followed. The shots were answered with rifle fire from the two lawmen on the other side of the street.

Bass rushed into the building, immediately rolling on the floor until he found a table to hide behind. He surveyed the room and saw nothing but customers trying to do anything they could to stay safe. Bass calculated three weapons were firing from the upstairs, none from downstairs.

Bass shouted, loud enough for those on the outside to hear. "All of you get to the door and get out of here!"

This was followed by a mad rush to the door, which was hurried by the continual gunfire coming from the upstairs room.

Now Bass worked his way to the other side of the room where he could get a good view of all that was taking place in the upstairs. His position proved not to be as advantageous as he had hoped. He decided to try to make it to the stairs and catch the men upstairs by surprise.

Before he could start his approach to the stairs, he heard women screaming and cussing from the upstairs. This caused him great concern.

Bass wondered what was taking place. Were the outlaws killing the women, or were they just frightened by all of the gunfire?

He decided that it was best to give it a few minutes to see what developed.

The gunfire continued, but the answer to Bass' question came in the form of one of the outlaws herding three of the ladies down the stairs. Their arms were tied together with bed sheets in a way that made them form a circle.

As they got to the bottom of the stairs, and before Bass could act, the outlaw stepped under one of the ladies arms and placed himself in the center of the circle, allowing him to be shielded by the women, both front and back.

Bass stayed behind the table, knowing it was impossible to attack this human fortress. Curious what the reaction would be, he shouted, "Why don't you just drop your gun and release those ladies?"

The outlaw turned toward Bass while placing his pistol against the head of one of the women. He said, "If'n you make one move, I'll kill these ladies, this one first. You better let me get out a here or their blood 'ill be on your head."

The man then pushed his shield toward the back door and exited.

The deputies stationed outside the door were now faced with the same restrictions that Bass had just encountered. They let the outlaw and his shield pass as he pushed and shoved the ladies toward the livery stable.

When the man left through the backdoor, Bass immediately ran out the front door and down the street to where he had left Blaze tied at a water trough. He tightened the cinch on Blaze and mounted him. He then rode out of the gunfire and to the adjoining street that led to the livery stable.

Once on the street to the livery stable, he slowed his pace, wanting to give the fugitive time to saddle up and, hopefully, release the women.

Bass didn't have to wait long before the door to the stable swung open, and the desperado exited with his horse in full stride.

Bass started his pursuit slowly. He saw no reason for gunfire in the city and knew that it would be only a matter of time before he would close the gap.

When they cleared town, Bass called on more speed from Blaze. Within moments, the outlaw turned to make sure he was clear. That's when he saw his efforts were fruitless. He pulled his pistol and fired a wild shot while in full gallop.

Bass pulled his horse to the left of the escaping man, making it nearly impossible for the fugitive to fire at him with his right hand. Nonetheless, the desperate outlaw continued to fire.

When Bass had counted six rounds, he leaned forward and told Blaze to move full speed. In less than a quarter of a mile, Blaze had Bass next to the fleeing fugitive.

Bass pulled his Winchester and brought it down sharply across the suspect's neck. The man fell forward, then off his saddle with a thud before bouncing across the frozen ground.

Bass pulled the unmanned horse to a stop and slowly returned to the fallen outlaw, who was still unconscious. Bass dismounted and manacled the man, then threw him over his saddle before manacling him to the cinch.

As Bass returned to town, he noticed the gunfire had stopped. He hoped this meant the lawmen had accomplished their mission. Just in case, he hurried to the livery stable and took a position where he could surprise anyone trying to enter.

After a few moments, he went to the front door and looked down the street. He was pleased to see the marshal and one of his deputies slowly walking toward the livery. Bass opened the door wider and waited for them to approach.

"How'd it go?" he asked when they were in talking range.

"They're both dead, and we need to get their horses to take their bodies back to Fort Smith. It's gonna be a sad trip 'cause we have to take Lewis' body, too. At least we put these bastards out of action. I see you got your man, and I hope he swings for all the trouble and misery he's caused," Marshal Upton said.

Chapter 19

Injustice

Bass continued to work for the marshal, and most of the cases were without much confrontation. When Bass was not working the Territory, he was completely occupied with the daily chores associated with the horses and his farm.

On an especially beautiful day, one that followed a night of light rain, Bass and Joseph were mucking the stable when a man on a great, gray gelding approached the house. Bass could see the man coming, so he leaned his fork against the stall wall and exited the stable, just as the man was dismounting in front of the house.

The rider was well dressed with the look of a successful business-man.

Bass rolled down his sleeves and tried to make himself more pre-sentable by dabbing his forehead with his handkerchief. He walked to the corral gate and said, "May I help you sir?"

The man turned from the porch steps with a broad smile on his face, and then began walking toward Bass. "I assume that you are Bass Reeves. I am Charles Pickens from Kansas," he said, extending his hand. "I have been told that you have some fine horses for sale. I am looking for a runner. I mean a real runner."

"Well sir, I sure will try to fit your needs," Bass said. "I won't try to kid you, but I think I have a young filly that shows me more speed than any I've bred. She is out of my famous English mare and by King, who is about as good as they come and, in my opinion, is as good as my original horse that has graced these parts. He's got production all over this country and most of 'em is better than their mamas. I know she has the blood, and she has showed me every sign of being all that her blood tells me she should be."

"Sounds like what I might be looking for," Pickens said. "Let's have a look at her."

They entered the stable, and Bass ushered the gentleman to the stall on the end. Bass entered, placed a halter on the big sorrel, then led her into the sunlight and the round pen before letting her loose.

The filly acted like she knew it was time to perform. She trotted around the circle, and then broke into a gallop. As she moved, she kicked her hind legs and tossed her head indicating that it was time for more room and more challenge. She continued to display the spirit and heart that Bass had described.

"Mr. Pickens, what do you think?"

"She looks right, and all you have told me about her heritage sounds good, but I would like to see her run," he said.

"Well, Mr. Pickens, that gelding you came in on sure looks like a fine feller. Why don't we just hook 'em up and see how she does," Bass proposed.

"I've had him in many a match race, and he's made me a nice sum of money," Pickens said, enjoying the verbal sparring. "We might be over-matching her."

"There ain't no way of findin' out just by talkin'," Bass said. "I'll tell you what I'll do. I want five hundred dollars for her, but if your horse can beat her, I'll take four, and if she beats 'im, I want six. How 'bout that?"

Pickens stroked his chin, then took off his broad-brimmed hat and wiped his head with his handkerchief. He replaced his hat and said, "I'll tell you what I'll do. If my gelding beats her, I'll give you three, and if she beats him, I'll give you six."

Bass now looked at the ground and scuffed his boot in the moist soil. He then looked up at the gray and thought for a moment.

"I think we've got a deal."

The two men shook hands. Pickens then went to the house, took his rifle and boot along with his saddlebags and placed them on the porch. He mounted the gray and went toward the corral.

While he was doing this, Bass was preparing the filly.

"Mr. Pickens, come with me, and I'll show you where we'll run."

They rode side-by-side to the flat land by the garden area. It was a long flat area, and the rain had made the soil conditions perfect for the race. The strip was more than a half-mile long, which the two rode, assessing the course. At the end, they turned and Bass said, "The first one to this flag wins."

Bass then put the filly in a slow lope back to the starting line.

The gray pulled up beside him and both men looked at the other. Bass counted to three and slapped his rein against the filly, which shot out into the lead.

Both mounts were pounding the ground, staying neck and neck at about an eighth of a mile. Then Bass let up on the filly and held her at a steady gait. The gray started to pull away, and Bass fell in behind. He kept the distance reasonable, and at a little past the quarter mile, he applied the whip.

The filly responded like he anticipated. She closed the distance in a short time, continuing to gain speed as she passed the gray. By the time they reached the flag, she had the big gray by two full lengths.

As he brought the filly to a halt, he could hear Pickens laughing. The laughter grew louder as he approached. Bass became concerned that the man was going to back out of the gentleman's agreement.

Instead, Pickens slapped Bass on the back, still wearing a broad grin on his face. "My good man, I may have lost the race, but I have gained the best runnin' horse I've ever seen. This may be the first time you have ever seen a loser happier than he was before the bet."

"What you gonna do with her Mr. Pickens?" Bass asked.

"Well, I was sent out to buy a runner for a lady named Belle Reed, and I probably will sell the filly to her. But before I deliver her, I'll probably pick up a few races in on my way back to Kansas," Pickens said.

"She should do you some good, and I wish you well," Bass said.

Pickens, with a smile still on his face, happily paid his bill. Pleased with his luck, he took the reins of the filly and departed, still singing as he turned and waived to Bass.

***

About an hour later, Bass again was distracted from his chores, this time by someone he knew, Marshal Upton.

The marshal pulled up to the house, and again, Bass straightened his clothing as he left the stable and walked to meet his friend.

"Marshal, good to see you. Are you here because there's more work to do?"

"Not this time. I was in the area checking on my deputies, and I just thought that it was proper for me to come out and let you know what has taken place. First thing, those two bastards that we caught in Wagoner are free."

"Did they escape?" Bass asked.

"Hell, I wish they had so I could go and get them and put them in a grave before they had a chance to buy their freedom. No, they along with several others bribed Judge Story. Their defense was that they did not fire at us except in self-defense. They claimed that the murder of Lewis, Mathews and Clarkson were done by those two we killed and that they were just innocent bystanders. A totally stupid defense, but the judge ruled that it was logical and set them free.

"Now, if this had been the only case like this, you might have just thought they were lucky. But, there have been several like this that were just as crazy, all under the jurisdiction of Judge Story. An investigation has been started to get to the bottom of these strange cases," the marshal said.

"They tell me that there will be a new judge appointed by President Grant soon. I only hope that he will be a man of honesty and justice. Until that happens, we're in a real fix. The murders are increasin' and the good for nothin' bastards just seem to be multiplyin' in the Territory. I'm not sure that it is worth the time and possible death of more of my men to send 'em into the Territory," Marshal Upton continued, getting more agitated as he spoke.

"Does sound like you is in a real fix," Bass sympathized. "When do you think a new judge will come to Fort Smith?"

"I hope soon. The jail is full, and if we don't get a judge soon, most of them will be let out 'cause they have the right to a speedy and just trial."

"Well, marshal, you caught 'em once, and if they lets 'em go, you just gonna have to do it again," Bass said.

"I know me and my men get paid to do that," Marshal Upton said. "But, it sure seems like a waste of time and work, not to mention the danger involved. Bass, do you realize that in the past few years, I have lost over forty good deputies to the no-goods in the Territory? It ain't no place for the weak at heart, and when you go in there you have a great chance of not comin' out standin' up."

"Marshal, I appreciate you stoppin' by and tellin' me what is hap-penin'," Bass said. "I hope you get some relief soon, and when you do, let me know. You know I'm ready and willin' to do anythin' that needs doin'."

**

In less than a month, Marshal Upton returned. He was riding upright in his saddle, and he had a look about him that gave Bass the impression that things were going better for him.

Bass sure hoped that was the case, because he had not been called to assist with any tracking jobs for several weeks. This, of course, had given him time to increase the garden area and do several things around the home place that Jennie and Mama wanted done, but Bass was really miss-ing the action and was getting cabin fever, even though planting time was nearing.

As the two men came face to face, Marshal Upton smiled and said, "Bass, things have really changed, and I have come here on official business.

You have been ordered to appear before Judge Isaac Parker in Fort Smith by Friday of this week."

Bass gave the marshal a questioning look as he asked, "Why are you smilin'? It sounds serious to me."

"Well, it really wasn't an order. It's really a request. The judge wants to talk to you 'bout becomin' a U.S. Marshal."

Bass tried to absorb what he was hearing. In a few minutes, he asked, "How could that be? There ain't no black men workin' for you now."

"I know there have been some Negro deputies up north, but none on this side of the Mississippi, and I am proud to say that I told the judge that if there was one man, black or white, that I would like to have work with me, it would be you.

"He has been authorized to hire up to two hundred men to clean up the Territory, and I told him that you could do the work of twenty. This, of course, got his attention, and when I told him that you was black, he seemed to like the idea more," the marshal continued.

"Now, I had to tell him about your run-in with the law a while back, but when I said that it was because you kicked the hell out of three rebs that was trying to molest a white girl and that you had been cleared of the charges, he really got excited.

"Let me tell you how this thing will work, if you're interested," the marshal said, continuing as Bass nodded at him. "You will be given a wagon and a cook. You'll have to pay the cook twenty dollars a month out of your take. You can take as many posse men as you think you'll need, and you will always need at least one. You pay them three dollars a day. You will get ten cents a mile both ways and seventy-five cents a day per prisoner to feed 'em. If you do your job, you can make over a hundred dollars a month, but if you really work at it, you can make lots more.

"Now, once you cross over the St. Louis and San Francisco Railroad, you is on your own. But, as good as you are, I know you will do a good job and make some good money while you're at it. The court will give you a bunch of warrants for people to pick up, and, of course, you can arrest anyone you catch breakin' the law while you're at it."

Bass thought a minute, and then asked, "What's a warrant?"

"It's a piece of paper that gives you the name of a man and what he is wanted for, and it gives you the authority to arrest that person," the marshal explained.

"Marshal, do you know I can't read?" Bass asked.

"I knew that, and often wondered why a guy that can speak four languages and read the ground like it's a book can't read," the marshal said.

"I've tried and tried hard, but the letters keep changin', and I just never could get 'em to make sense to me," Bass said, somewhat embarrassed.

"Well, I'm not bothered 'bout that," the marshal assured him. "As smart as you are and the way you know the land, you will figure out a way to handle that. I told him that you being black and having worked so much with the Indians that you could get to places and find people that no white man could. Now, are you gonna see the judge on Friday?"

Bass looked at the ground for a moment, then took his hat off and looked inside of it, as if the answer were written there. He replaced his hat, smiled at the marshal and said, "Tell 'im I'll be there. We can at least talk. I ain't never met a big-time judge, and that might be worth the trip."

Marshal Upton nodded, and then began to mount his horse to leave, adding, "Bass, if you come, bring your gear. If'n you take the job, we have a pile of warrants and will want you on the road that day. Of course, I will be there and give you as much assistance as I can. I sure hope you take it 'cause the Territory is about to explode, and I can sure use your help."

Chapter 20

Pistol Pete

Bass had been to Fort Smith several times, but he had never seen a crowd this large, even on a Saturday. There were the regular farmers and cowboys, but there seemed to be more men dressed in suits than he could remember. He began to wonder if he had misread his calendar and had come on Sunday rather than Monday.

He headed to the marshal's office, where a young man who looked no more than thirteen years old greeted him. Despite his youthful look, the young man was carrying side arms as if he knew how to use them, and he was sporting a shiny deputy marshal's badge.

While his youth caused doubt, the energy he displayed was impressive. The thing that struck Bass immediately was the young man's eyes. They were not natural. They seemed to each focus in a different direction. The longer Bass looked at them, the more uncomfortable he became. He tried not to look into his face, but he couldn't seem to avoid it.

The young man stuck out his hand and said, "Welcome. I assume you are Bass Reeves. I was told you would be comin'. They asked me to show you over to the judge's chambers as soon as you got here. I am Frank, Frank Eaton, but most people call me either Sir or Pistol Pete."

Bass smiled as he took the young man's hand in his and applied a firm grip. "Well, Mister Pete, I am glad to meet you. Tell me, Sir, how'd you get such a handle?"

"It seems that there ain't much doubt that I am the fastest and best shot with a pistol in these parts," the self-assured young man said. "A few didn't believe that, and they ain't around to answer the question. However, I have heard you're a pretty good hand with that thing. I'm glad we're on the same side, and we won't have to match up or nothin'," Pistol Pete said, putting on his hat. "Let's hurry on over. The judge is havin' a meetin', but told me not to dilly-dally around when you got here."

As they headed toward the courthouse, Bass asked, "I have been here a few times but never saw so many folks millin' around. Is somethin' notable happenin'?"

"You mean you ain't heard? We had us one hell of a hangin' the other day. Yes sir, one hell of a hangin'. Strung up five no goods, all at one time. There were over five thousand people here to see that event and lots of 'em was from as far away as New York town. Lots of 'em reporter fellers stayed around to talk with folks and just tried to breath in the air," the young Pistol Pete said, showing great excitement talking about the event.

"They've already started callin' Judge Parker, 'The Hangin' Judge.' Lots of 'em Yankees has been sayin' it was too harsh and brutal, but they ain't rode in the Territory, and they sure ain't never lived with the bastards that roam there. The folks from this area are tickled that someone has started enforcin' the law."

Entering the courthouse was a real surprise to Bass. It was not a huge room, about as big as some saloons he had seen. But it was clean and showed an exceptional sign of order. A short fence divided the room between an area where the people sat and an area with two tables and the place where the judge sat. The judge's area was raised so he was looking down on all that he controlled. The ceiling sported a multi-globed lamp, that had the look of elegance.

Pete took Bass through the swinging doors of the low fence. The pair walked across the court area, directly to a door on the far side of the room. Pete rapped on the door and, on command of a voice from inside the room, pushed the door open. After he entered, he motioned for Bass to step inside.

The small room was crowded, and it was evident from the looks on the attendants' faces that some serious conversation was taking place.

Marshal Upton stood and motioned for Bass to join the group. The marshal began making introductions.

"Bass Reeves, I would like for you to meet Judge Parker, U.S. Attorney Clayton and George Maledon, the official executioner for this district.

Bass smiled as he extended his hand to each, noting that his great mustache was no match for the adornment sported by Clayton and Maledon. Clayton had a magnificent set of chin whiskers, and Maledon's face was covered with so much brush that he looked like he was wearing camouflage.

Maledon also was sporting two handle-forward pistols in his belt, which made him look like he was ready and able to carry out his executions personally, as easily as he did on the gallows.

They all extended their hands and nodded to Bass. The judge rose from behind his desk and said, "Mr. Reeves, I hope you have come here for me to swear you in as a U. S. Deputy Marshal. I have heard many good things about you, and the marshal here tells me he needs you and your skills. There is little doubt that your government needs you."

The statement "that your government needs you" rang in Bass' ear. He had never heard his name and the government mentioned in the same sentence. He was there to accept the position, but if he had ever questioned his decision, the judge's declaration left no doubt in Bass' mind.

"Sir, Judge Parker, I've come for the job," Bass said.

"I, then, will swear you in, and, as soon as that is over, I want you and the marshal to join Pete, who'll get you lined out. I have a big responsibility to the people and President Grant, and I want all the manpower I can get to get it accomplished. May I add that it is with great pride that I am swearing a Negro in as an officer of the law? You will be the first of your race west of the Mississippi to wear the badge of U.S. Marshal. I know you will make me proud."

After the very brief ceremony, the judge extended his hand and firmly grasped Bass' hand. With a big smile, he placed his left hand on top of Bass'. The warmth that Bass felt from the firmness of the grip assured the new deputy that Judge Parker's words were not just idle statements.

"Bass, how old are you?" the judge asked.

"I figure I am about 'bout forty, Sir Judge."

"Bass, all you have to do is address me as 'Judge' or 'Your Honor,'" Judge Parker explained. "Now, the reason I asked your age is that I'm wondering if it would bother you to take some instructions from a young whipper-snapper like Pete here. I know he looks like a kid, but he's a little older than he looks, and he has had a lot of experience that could be of service to you in the future. So, if you don't mind listening to a youngster, I will assign him to help get you started."

"You know Judge, all my life I've looked and listened to 'bout everyone I've had a chance to meet, and usually I learned somthin' every time. If'n you think he is the right man, I'd gladly be more than welcome to take his advice," Bass said.

"Well, with that settled, I am assigning Pete to work with you 'till you get your feet on the ground," the Judge said. "Pete, you will help Bass get his crew together and outfit the group. And while you're at it, give the man some advice on how we work. I would also like for you to accompany him on at least his first trip into the Territory. From what I have heard, there is no reason to spend any time on describing the Territory — he probably knows it and the people better than anyone I have sent in there."

Pete smiled and said, "Yes, Judge, I understand."

The men rose. The marshal and the others again extended their hands and welcomed Bass into their prestigious assemblage.

Bass followed Pete out of the courthouse and down to the area where all the outfitting for the U.S. Marshal Service was done.

Pete said, "You need a wagon and a team. Joseph here will help you put them together. I'll go see who is available to cook and try to find you a posse man that you can depend on."

Joseph extended his rough and calloused hand to Bass and said, "Let's get you started. Come with me."

They went to the back of the stable and entered a holding pen with horses.

Bass stood for a moment, assessing the livestock before asking, "You got any mules?"

"I got mules," Joseph said. Is that what you want?"

"Is any of 'em broke to ride?" Bass asked.

"Got one, but you better be a rider. She bucks some. She also is a kicker. Don't touch her left flank or she will kick the livin' daylights outta you or anything behind 'er. If you touch 'er real hard, she kicks with both feet, and it is like lightin'. I seen 'er kick a hole in the side of the barn and was jest glad I was not standin' in 'er way."

"Sounds like I had better be right careful with 'er," Bass said. "Have you got a mate for her?"

"That big gray works with 'er jest fine," Joseph said.

"Then that's the team I want," Bass said, liking what he saw and heard.

The two men inspected the wagons before Bass made his choice. They then went to work greasing the axles and preparing the wagon for the task ahead.

Pete later came in, smiling.

"Joseph, you won't believe it, but ol' Newly said he was wantin' to come back to work. Said he had all the town life and bein' cooped up with his wife he could stand. He's ready to go if'n Bass wants 'im."

Joseph turned to Bass and said, "You is in luck. He's the best cook in the business, makes biscuits that melt in your mouth. On top of that, he is pretty good at handlin' prisoners, just as good as a posse man, as far as that goes. You better grab 'im."

"Why's he not workin' now?" Bass asked.

"He was workin' with Marshal Howard — been doin' it for quite a spell — but the marshal got waylaid last month," Joseph said. "It shook Newly up. They not only worked together, but were really good friends. I think he just decided that it wasn't worth it, and wanted to try somethin' not so dangerous. But, you know, I work with all these fellers, and it seems that once you get in the hunt, it becomes part of your life, and few ever stop unless a bullet takes 'em out."

Pete joined in, "I'll stop as soon as I finish my job."

Bass thought for a moment before asking, "Can Newly read?"

This stopped both men from saying more. They looked at each, definitely trying to think about an answer.

After some moments of searching, Pete said, "Newly has got some learnin', and I remember that he was readin' the paper when I went to his house, so the answer is yes. Why do you care?"

Bass replied, "Just wanted to know, and I'll take 'im. Tell 'im to get to the store and start puttin' all the things he needs together. He surely knows what we need. When he gets that done, have 'im meet here with me. I'll be around here most of the time. In fact, I think I'll sleep here 'till we hit the trail."

***

The morning was pleasant, and Pete showed up just in time to join Bass and Joseph for coffee. There was something extra peaceful about a hot cup of coffee boiled over the extreme heat of the forge. As they sat and enjoyed their cups of brew, the men exchanged stories. In these moments, Bass began to feel part of something, something that had meaning and that could lead to a companionship in the sharing of a challenge that few men would ever know.

Later, waiting in the back, leaning against the stable wall, soaking up the warm morning sun, Ed, the posse man that Pete had told to come and talk with Bass about the job, arrived.

Ed had worked as a posse man many times, and the description of what he had done and how he worked pleased Bass. The fact that both Pete and Joseph had spoken highly of him carried even more weight. Bass also was pleased that Ed never seemed to notice or care that Bass was black.

Bass hired Ed on the spot, telling him that anything he needed to do before they left, he had better get it done.

While they were waiting for all the supplies to arrive, Pete said to Bass, "You asked me why they call me Pistol Pete. Would you like for me to show you?"

Bass looked at him and grinned because he knew there was no reason to say no, and even if he did, Pete would probably show him anyway.

"Sure Pete. I just can't wait to see what you can do," Bass said, smiling.

With this encouragement, Pete pushed himself away from the wall and flexed his right hand. After he had done this a few times, he reached for his pistol, rapidly pulling it from his holster several times. Each time he did, the motion seemed to get faster and smoother. He then reached into his front pocket and pulled out a silver dollar. He looked at it for a few moments, then in one smooth motion, tossed it into the air. At the same time, he pulled his pistol, cocked it and fired a round.

The dollar radically changed directions in mid-air. It sailed across the corral area, landing next to the fence.

Pete walked to the spot and retrieved the coin. He turned and walked back toward Bass with a broad smile on his face. About ten feet from Bass, he flipped the coin toward Bass, who caught it in flight. Bass looked at the coin, noting a corner that had been chipped off.

When Bass looked up, the smile on Pete's face reminded Bass of a puppy that had just fetched a boot. Pete obviously wanted Bass' approval and praise.

Bass simply stood there.

Pete, finally, in a frustrated tone said, "Well, can you do that?"

Bass calmly stated, "Never tried. Never had a dollar to waste. But, it sure looks like it would come in handy if someone ever starts thowin' dollars at you."

Pete was at a loss for words. He always got looks of amazement from people who saw his shooting. Then he noticed a broad smile spreading across Bass' face, followed by Bass beginning to laugh before saying, "Very impressive. Thanks for the lesson. I know not to ever draw on you."

Bass then reached his long, powerful arm out, placing his hand on Pete's shoulder. "If I ever need a backup, I hope you're there."

The young man now smiled, apparently pleased that he had impressed a man with a reputation for being one of the best guns in the Territory.

"Now," Bass said to the young man. "Tell me your story. I noticed that you said that you're through when your job's done. For a feller that has a particular skill like that, what does the end of the job mean?"

Pete looked at the ground for a moment before raising his eyes toward Bass' inquiring stare. He took a deep breath before saying, "When I was eight, some Confederates — at least that is what they claimed to be in the war, but they were really a pack of murderin' low lifes that rode with Quantrill — anyways, they was raisin' hell in Kansas, and my papa was one of the fellers who was tryin' to bring peace to the area. The word went out, and one night these bushwackin' sons-of-bitches caught my papa alone. I saw it happen. They killed him in cold blood. He didn't even have a gun. He was comin' back from the privy. I didn't know all of their names, but I knew some of 'em, and I learned the others. My papa's friend told me that I would be no count if I didn't make 'em pay for what they did to Papa.

"He took me right then and there and taught me how to shoot. By the time I was fifteen, I had found one of 'em and made 'em pay the price. I put four in his hide before he could hit the ground. I found out later that another of 'em had got killed in a gunfight over a card game. So, I figured I had better hit the trail if'n I was gonna do what I had to do. I decided that I had to get a job that would keep me movin' and workin' with guns," Pete said, losing any initial reluctance to talk.

"I went to the Territory and looked for the other four, but ran outta money. So, I tried to join the army at Fort Gibson. I lied about my age, but they could tell I was a lyin'. It made me so out a sorts that I told the colonel that I could out do anyone at the fort. He thought that was the funniest yarn he'd ever heard. I finally told him that I would challenge anyone in the fort and that if I won; he had to let me stay and work on the grounds for a week.

"Well, he called out one of the troopers, and we had a little contest. I beat him bad, and it really got the colonel's goat. He then told me that he had another trooper, his champion, and that if I beat him, I could stay for a month.

I put him away nearly as fast as the other. So, I hung around the place for a while, and, finally, he put out the word to other forts. The officers would bet against me. I guess the colonel figured out that he could make money on my shootin'. From what I figured, he made a pretty good chunk of change off of me.

"That's when the colonel started callin' me Pistol Pete, and it just stuck. He never even introduced me as anything other than Pistol Pete to those that came in to try to best me. All the others started callin' me the same.

"The colonel finally told me about the U.S. Marshal Service. So, I went to Van Buren, and with his recommendation, got a job doin' this. Like I said, this work suits me just fine, but my real purpose is to find the remainin' murderin' bastards that killed my papa. When I get that done, I'll just bide my time till somethin' comes up. I'll find 'em for sure. Now, if you ever get a warrant for a Campsey or a Ferber, save it for me. These are the bastards I be lookin' for," Pete said, concluding his story.

"Well, sounds like you are on your way to findin' 'em, and if'n I do run across one of 'em, I'll try to save 'em for you," Bass promised, remembering a time when he had nursed very similar feelings. "I hope you get 'em 'fore they get you. That said, have you ever had a close call?"

Pete nodded yes and began, "One time I was workin' up by the Kansas line and had these two fellers trapped in a dugout. They were puttin' up a pretty good fight," Pete said. "I noticed that there was smoke comin' out of the chimney, so I had my posse man train a lot of firepower on the door while I went around and put a blanket over the chimney. Well, it didn't take much time at all before the two fellers came out with their rifles in the air, chokin' for breath. I was still on the roof and told 'em to throw their rifles down, which they did. They was makin' such a fuss that I was sure they were occupied just tryin' to get a breath, so I started to crawl down off the dugout. But, while I had my back turned, one of 'em pulled a pistol out of his shirt, and just as I turned around, he fired point blank at me.

"The slug hit me square in the chest and knocked me back against the wall of the dugout. I knew I was dead or surely gonna die. I decided that I didn't want to go alone, so I pulled my pistol and put one through his eye.

"When I finally got my breath, I reached into my shirt and found that the slug had hit square into a cross that a young lady I had been seein' had given me just the week before. I had a hell of a bruise — it took me about a month before the blue went away — but I was no worse for the wear.

"I have said since that day that I'd rather have the prayers of a good woman in a fight than half a dozen hot guns. If'n she's talkin' to headquarters, that carries more weight than any .45 " Pete said.

"Sounds like somethin' my mama would sure agree with," Bass said. "She always says that the Lord will take care of you when the need comes along."

Later, Newly arrived, and it was agreed that he and Ed would be Bass' first team for his entry into Indian Territory as a U.S. lawman. Pete said he was going to tag along and try to assist, but would probably be parting ways as soon as he felt Bass had things under control. They all agreed to depart the next morning.

Chapter 21

The New Lawman

Bass and his party started with the rising sun. As they rode, Bass noticed that he felt differently than he had in the past. He now realized that he had taken on a great responsibility and that the things he was about to encounter were going to make a difference in the Territory.

He really did not have any apprehension as to his ability, but he had never acted with the full authority of the law, and it did feel special. Bass' concern, above all, was to avoid bringing disgrace to him or the law that he had sworn to uphold. He made a promise to himself that he would enforce the law, conducting his business with honor and dignity.

Bass asked Pete, "When you first went into the Territory, how did you feel?"

Pete thought for a while and responded, "Like I was ten feet tall. I was jest a kid, but I knew there was no man that could equal me, and I knew I had the brass to make it happen. I was jest like you, in that I had a more experienced marshal along, but I wanted to prove that the Judge had made the right decision when he swore me in. Of course, in the back of my mind, I was really thinkin' that I now had the power to bring down my Pa's killers with whatever means I chose."

As they approached the railroad, Pete said, "This here is the dead line. It means that once you cross it, you is on your own, and all of the world you meet from here on out is out to kill you. You never trust anyone you don't know, and even those you know, you need to be leery of. That star on your chest draws enemies like fresh horse droppin's draw flies. There're good people in here, but you'll learn that most everybody has somethin' to hide, and the only time they're glad to see you is when they need you."

"Sounds a little troublin'," Bass said. "Where do you set up your first camp?"

"I like to swing up to the edge of the Chickasaw Nation and set up there. I then make a swing out in each direction for a day or two and see what I can learn or run across. Newly knows all that needs to be done in camp, and he can handle anything. We can swing out together in the mornin'."

"Then let's do that," Bass said. "I got to get with Newly tonight and do some figurin' on what persons I want on the warrant list."

***

Before the break of dawn, Newly was on his way to set up camp, while Pete, Ed and Bass began their journey. With Pete's advice, the trio headed toward Wewoka. The trail was well used and they made good time. They topped a hill and observed two men in a wagon ahead of them. It was apparent that the load was quite heavy with their team laboring hard.

As the trio approached the driver, he and his companion started to act a little uneasy. Their behavior could be explained by the fact that no one in the Territory could trust anyone, or it could be that they had something to hide.

Bass rode up beside the wagon, bidding the men a friendly hello before asking, "What you got here?"

"We ain't got nothin'," one of the men said.

"Well, your team seems to disagree. They're sure workin' hard to be pullin' nothin'. Let me see what you got in there."

"Ain't got time to let nobody see. Gotta get on down the road," the man said.

"How 'bout if a U.S. Marshal asked you to have a look? Would that change your mind?" Bass asked.

"Is you a marshal?" the man asked.

"That's right, and I now want a see what you've got that's makin' them horses work so hard," Bass said, showing his badge.

The teamster pulled the team up and looked down at the floor of the wagon before saying, "I is jest doin' my job. I was told to take this wagon to a man in Wewoka, and that is all I is doin'."

"Who told you to take it to what man?" Bass asked.

"A feller in Fort Smith gave me ten dollars and told me to take it to a guy named Jim Davies in Wewoka, and that is all's I's doin'. Marshal, I got a wife and three hungry kids, and I needed the ten dollars real bad. I know what's in this wagon, but I had to have the money for my kids to eat," the man said.

"What's your name and have you ever been in trouble with the law before?" Bass asked.

"I's Wilber Martin. This here is my boy Robin, and, no sir, I ain't never been in trouble. I sharecropped for ten years down by Atoka ways. Then my wife got sick, so I had to take 'er to Fort Smith, and things jest got worser and worser. This is the first time I had a chance to make some money since I went broke in the city payin' for the doctor."

"Wait here a minute," Bass said, before turning and riding back to Pete and Ed, where they were waiting behind the wagon.

"Either one of you know this man?" Bass asked.

"I've seen him in Atoka once or twice. I think he is a sodbuster from around there," Ed said.

"He ever been in trouble?" asked Bass.

"Na, just a sodbuster. They ain't got time to get in no trouble," Ed said.

Bass rode back to the front of the wagon and said, "Here is what's gonna happen. You walk into town and tell Mr. Davies that the wagon is in them woods over there, broke down. Tell 'im he needs to bring a team and some men to move the barrels. Your boy stays here. You do this, and I'll let you and the boy go home. Now do this quick, you understand?"

Wilber hit the ground running. Bass told the boy to get up in the woods with the wagon. At the same time he reached into his saddlebag and handed the boy a biscuit and some jerky. He reassured the boy that he and his dad would have no problems, if his dad did what he was told.

Feeling confident, Bass told Pete that he might as well go on and make some rounds in Wewoka. He and Ed would wait with the wagon and handle this matter.

In about an hour, a wagon with four men came down the road. The men obviously were looking for the wagon in the woods. When they spotted it, they hurriedly pulled their wagon next to it and rapidly started transferring the barrels of whiskey into their wagon.

When the task was complete, Ed and Bass came out from their cover, guns drawn, and announced that the men were all under arrest for dealing whiskey in the Territory. Bass had one of the men open a barrel. Both Bass and Ed had a taste to confirm their suspicions. Then, while Davies and his men watched in horror, Bass poured the contents of all the barrels on the ground.

When he was through, Bass instructed Wilber and his boy to get in the wagon, head back to Fort Smith and take care of his wife. Before he sent them on their way, he made Mr. Davies give Wilber ten dollars. As he was leaving, Bass told Wilber to contact Joseph at the outfitting station, that there might be some work there for him.

Bass told Ed to take the prisoners to the base camp and have Newly confine them. Then Ed was to meet Bass back in Wewoka that evening.

Bass planned to do some scouting in the area and, hopefully, come up with more prisoners for him.

***

Bass rode north for a distance before encountering a group of Indians coming down the road. He introduced himself, in the Seminole language, as a U.S. Marshal. When he got no response, he spoke in Cherokee. One of the men responded.

The one who seemed to be the spokesman for the group nodded his head upon hearing Bass' name and responded, "I am Kenneth Long Knife, and I know of you. I know that you've been a friend of the Indians for years. When did you become a marshal?"

"Just this week," Bass said.

"I hope you will help clean out all these bad men who have come and trampled on us," Long Knife said. "You know they've cheated us out of our homes and farms back East, and now they've allowed this plague of murderers to infest what little the white man has left us. If you are really here to help, you can begin by catching the five that killed my white neighbor, Andy Beckum, a good man, killed just the other day. I understand the killers are somewhere near Wewoka and are bragging about how they have nothing to fear."

"Tell me what they look like, and I promise you that I'll make an honest stab at making them pay. Let me tell you that any problems you and your people have should be reported, and I will do everythin' I can to help your Light Horse Police, if needed. You know that I can't get involved in problems between Indians, but I sure intend to ride herd on all the others."

Bass got descriptions of the accused. Bidding the Indians goodbye, he immediately turned Blaze and put him in full stride toward Wewoka. He had planned to be there by evening, but with this news, he felt that he had no time to waste.

Blaze had not been pushed for some time. The horse seemed to enjoy the test, willingly putting his effort into the run. Before long, Bass could see Wewoka in the distance. He slowed Blaze to a gallop and finally eased him to a walk before they reached the outskirts of the town.

Once in town, Bass started looking for Pete's horse before finding it tied near the general store. He pulled Blaze to a halt, dismounted and entered the store. He looked around, and then asked the clerk if he had seen the man on the horse tied out front.

The clerk nodded his head and pointed across the street toward the saloon.

Bass crossed the street quickly and peered over the swinging doors
before entering. He saw Pete in the far corner, sitting at a table with two
men, all appearing to be in a social conversation. Bass entered slowly.

When Pete noticed Bass, he immediately motioned for him to join the
group. Pete introduced his companions as friends who had helped him in
the past. He told them that Bass would be covering the countryside now.

The men's faces showed great surprise, shock and even a raised eye-
brow, at being introduced to a black man, especially one wearing the badge
of a U.S. Marshal.

Bass said, "I am glad to meet you fellers, and it's possible that we
can begin with some information on five fellers that probably were in here
earlier. Pete, I just got word that they killed a feller named Beckum just the
other day."

The two men looked shocked, with one asking, "Andy Beckum?"

"That's the name I got," Bass said. "Did you know 'im?"

"Sure. He was a hell of a feller, never caused no problem and always
was willin' to help if he could," the man said. "I sure hate to hear about him
gettin' killed. What can we do to help?"

"Did you see the fellers I just talked about?"

"There were five in here a little earlier, and I think I heard 'em say
they were heading toward Seminole. Since it's gettin' dark, I'll bet they is
gonna stop someplace between here and there."

"Got any idea where that might be?"

Pete said, "There ain't but a few places that it could be, and I know
'em all. Let's head out now, and we can check 'em out as we go."

Bass felt an urge for caution. "Pete, let's wait for Ed. He should be
here in a bit. I think we'll need 'im."

After Ed arrived, the men quickly departed toward Seminole. The
trail was well lit by a full moon, and they moved as hastily as they could.

The first cabin they approached was lit by a lamp and all seemed
quirt and in order. So, they hurried over the trail.

The approach to the second was much different. There was the familiar glow of a lamp through the window, but it was noticeable that the corral
had far more horses in it than one would expect.

Pete said in a low whisper, "This is Carl Fowler's place. He lives here
alone, since his wife and kids went back East. There is no reason for all the
horses. They must be here. There definitely is somethin' wrong. Carl has a
big dog that always makes a ruckus when people approach."

Bass quickly took charge of the situation, saying, "Let's wait until
they're sturrin' in the mornin' and see what takes place. For now, Ed, you
take the ten-gauge and sneak around to the back door. Make sure you have

plenty of rounds with you. Take your rifle, too. We may be in for a real fight. I want you to make sure these guys don't get out a there. From the light coming from the windows, I think I can get over by the outhouse and cover both the front and back door, if needed. Pete, you take the front. As soon as anyone comes out that door, Pete, you'll call 'em out. We'll have to play it from there. Sorry, but looks like it's going to be a long night, fellers."

The men did not look disappointed. They quickly took their positions and settled in for the wait.

In the morning light the cabin was silent, and as the shadows started to shorten, movement could be heard in the cabin. The back door of the cabin opened and a man stumbled out the door. He was still in his long johns and had no weapon on him. He carefully stepped in his bare feet toward the outhouse.

Bass motioned to Ed to let him pass. Then Bass slid behind the out-house.

The man stopped as he reached the facility and placed an out-stretched hand against the building so he could brush the pebbles from his feet before entering.

Bass quickly stepped around the corner, pointing his Colt in the man's face as he cocked the hammer.

"Now sir, if you would be so kind as to step to the back, I have a surprise for you."

The man's eyes widened before he began trying to wipe the sleep from his eyes, as if he were dreaming.

"If you make a sound, it'll be the last one you hear except for the blast from this pistol."

The man quickly became fully awake and followed the instructions.

Bass motioned for him to sit on the ground, by a young oak tree. With the man's arms around the trunk of the tree, Bass placed manacles on his wrists, thereby securing the man to the spot.

"Now just set still and keep quiet or you'll wish you had," Bass in-structed. "I've got more business to do."

Moments later, another half-dressed man appeared at the back door and shouted, "Joe, hurry up. We need some more wood for the stove." He stood for a moment, looking toward the outhouse.

"Joe, what the hell is you doin'? We need that wood now!" he again demanded.

At this moment, Ed stood with the shotgun pointed at the man-in-need-of-firewood and said, "That's enough. You're under arrest. Get over here."

The startled man rushed for the open door. Ed pulled the trigger.

The blast of the ten-gauge shattered the still of the morning air while the side of the door exploded with the buckshot. The man hit the floor of the cabin, crawling inside. The leg of his long johns was already showing traces of blood, as the door slammed behind him.

Ed fired another round, hitting the center of the door and blowing massive splinters of wood in all directions.

At nearly the exact moment, Pete's rifle cracked from the side of the ridge. He fired rapidly, answered with pistol fire from the house.

Pete then hollered, "This is the law, and we are here to take you fellers in, one way or the other!"

Pete's words were quickly followed by more pistol fire from the house, then the crack of rifle fire.

Pete again hollered, "You're makin' a poor choice. I can see you comin' out of there feet first. Now throw them shootin' irons out and make it easy for everyone."

"We ain't comin' out, and if you want us, you is gonna hav'ta come in, lawman," one of the men in the cabin yelled before he and the others began firing again.

Pete answered with a rapid release of rifle fire that was backed up by Ed again firing both barrels of his shotgun into the door, which now fell off one of its hinges, leaving the doorway only half covered.

Through the door opening, Bass let fly a round from his Winchester, followed by two more rounds while Ed was reloading for his next attack.

In a short time, the valley was filled with smoke and the continual explosion of gunfire. Then the cabin fell silent.

Both Ed and Bass sent rounds through the now completely open back door. At the same time, Pete sent projectiles through the two windows in the front of the cabin.

There was no response from the cabin, until a voice shouted out, "We've had enough. Stop your shootin'. We is comin' out."

Bass rushed to a position where he had full view of the front of the cabin. He sighted on the front door and shouted, "Throw your guns out the front door first. Then come out one at a time with your hands in the air."

The guns came out like a flush of quail, and then there was silence.

"Now, don't be fools. Come on out like I told you," Bass ordered.

Slowly, each man appeared as demanded. All of them were in their long johns, and they all had blood running from different parts of their bodies. It looked as though none had received a direct hit, but the bullets and projectiles that had glanced around the cabin had all found their mark, one way or another.

They were all manacled and given their retrieved clothing and boots from the house. During the retrieval of the clothing, the body of poor Carl Fowler was found lying in the corner of the cabin. The only good thing, Bass thought, was that his other family members weren't there, or they most certainly would have joined him in his eternal rest.

Bass went to the corral to retrieve the men's horses and prepare for the trip back to the holding wagon. While gathering the saddles, he saw a large white dog lying on the barn floor. At first he was sure the dog was as dead as his master. There was blood running from his head, and he made no movement. However, when Bass passed him again with the second saddle, he thought he saw his chest move. Bass stood for a moment over the downed animal. Yes, the big critter was breathing.

Bass first thought that he might as well put a bullet in him to end his suffering, but then reconsidered. There was something about the large canine that attracted Bass. He did not know why, but he felt this animal had suffered enough, and that it should be his duty to try and save him.

Bass picked up the animal and carried him out of the barn. He drew some water from the well and washed the blood from the dog's head and stroked him from head to tail. The dog finally started to respond while Bass began placing some water on his dried tongue. Bass then cupped water in his massive hands and held it where the dog could drink.

After all of the prisoners were mounted, Bass placed the huge dog over Blaze's saddle and climbed to a position behind his new companion. As they made their way back to the holding wagon, Bass continued to stroke and massage the animal.

With time, the dog became a part of the parade, and Bass placed him on the ground and let him run with the group. When the dog showed signs of weakening, Bass would return him to his position on the saddle.

At the campsite, Bass had Newly feed the dog. And when they moved the base site, the dog rode in the wagon as the group made its way to all the stopping points Pete said they need to make.

Several days later, as Bass and Pete were following the procession, Pete asked, "What 're you gonna name your dog?"

Bass looked straight ahead and said, "I been givin' that a lot of thought, and after much ponderin', I think I've come up with the perfect name for the pot-licker."

He paused and then, with a smile on his face said, "His name is Dog."

Pete and Bass both broke out in laughter, and Pete slapped Bass on the shoulder.

Late in the afternoon, after Bass had returned to camp with two men whose names were on warrants Bass held, an Indian riding a horse came into the clearing. He stopped for a moment, observed the setting and then hesitantly spoke. He seemed to have trouble with the words in English, so Bass greeted him in Cherokee.

The man seemed to relax. In Cherokee, he told his story, "I was coming from town and had just delivered the last of all of my crops to the general store. While I was headed home, I came upon a camp on the creek about two miles south of here. There were three men in the camp, and they invited me in. All I wanted was to pass through, but they held up a bottle of whiskey, and I stopped to take a drink. While I was drinking, they pulled their pistols and told me that they wanted all of my money or they would kill me. I gave them all sixty dollars that I had, and that was all the money that I have to keep my family goin'. If you're really the law, I would be grateful if you would go down there and get my money. If you don't, my family will have a really hard time."

Bass replied in Cherokee, "Would you be willing to go back and show me where they are?"

"If you think you can get my money back, I'd do about anything. My wife is goin' to kill me if I come home without that money," the man said.

"Give me a minute, and we will see what this lawman can do for you," Bass said.

Bass went to the wagon and changed into an old baggy set of clothes. He changed his sharply polished boots into a pair that was run over and had holes in the soles. He carefully slipped into the old boot the .22 that he always carried. To complete his wardrobe, he grabbed a tattered hat that looked like it had been in a tornado.

Now in his new garb, he went to the big female mule and placed a withered saddle on her, mounted and said, "Let's go."

As he was leaving the camp, all of his companions were laughing uncontrollably at his new look. The change was so drastic for Bass — he always was the prime example of spit and polish — that the men couldn't help but find it comical.

The Cherokee man and Bass made their way south. As they approached the creek, they saw the glow of a fire.

Bass told his traveling companion, "You stay here. I'll handle this."

As he rode forward toward the camp, he began singing The Old Rugged Cross. As he and the mule came into the opening, the four men around the fire sat down their tins of beans and rose to their feet.

Bass stopped his singing and said, "Sorry fellas, but could yous spares a cup of coffee? I's been ridin' for some spell now and sure coulds use a warmin'."

The men looked at each other, and finally one said gruffly, "You got any money"?

"I gots a little. Why?" Bass, the impersonator, said innocently.

"We don't just give stuff away. If you want a cup, it will cost you two bits."

"Seems a might high, but I'll do it if'n you'll throws in a tin of 'em beans."

"Let's see your money," the man demanded.

Bass dismounted the mule and tied her to a tree. As he walked toward the fire, he pulled an old purse from his tattered pants and started fumbling with the contents. He finally pulled out a quarter and held it up so all could see.

"You got anymore in there?" the man asked.

"Maybe ten dollars. Why?"

"We just thought that you might be interested in a jug of whiskey for the road," the man said, now talking a bit more friendly.

"You gots whiskey?" Bass asked, appearing interested.

"We sure got ten dollars worth."

Bass reached into the purse again and pulled out ten dollars.

"Is that all you got there?" the man asked again.

"Sure is."

"Then why don't you just give us the purse and get back on that flea-bitten mule and get out of this camp," the man said, losing all pretenses.

"You means you's gonna takes my's money and purse?"

All of the men pulled their pistols and pointed them at Bass. "That's right," said the spokesman for the group as a snarl came from his lips and a imposing smile crossing his face.

"Glory be, I sures hates that, but I's sure glads you's not gonna takes my poke I hides on my mule," Bass said, secretly enjoying his act.

The men started to laugh and look at each other, before the talker said, "I know you darkeys is stupid, but I guess you is maybe the stupidest darkey I've ever seen. You stupid bastard, get over to that mule and fetch that poke."

Bass dropped his head and slowly moved toward the mule. He walked to her left side and started fumbling with the saddle, steadily increasing his speed in the search of the supposedly hidden poke. The longer he looked, the more frantic he became. Finally, the men started to become more agitated and moved closer to him.

When the talker reached just the right position, Bass drove his fist in the mule's left flank. The response was first a tremendous bray that was instantly followed by both hind legs leaving the ground and extending backward with the speed and sting of a bee.

When both hoofs made contact with the man, it sounded like dropping a ripe watermelon on a boardwalk. His feet left the ground and his arms were flapping in the air like a bird as he sailed backward. The force of his projection caused his body to crash into the man behind him forcing both of them into the glowing embers of the campfire.

When they hit the fire, sparks and embers raced toward the sky. This was followed by screams for help from the man that the talker had propelled into the gates of hell. The victim of the big mule's attack said nothing. He could not get his breath and seemed content to lie in the fire as his best option for the pain he was feeling.

The other two gunmen completely forgot about Bass and rushed to rescue their companions. Bass simply pulled up his loose fitting trouser leg and pulled his .22 from its hiding place. He slowly stepped forward and retrieved the pistol that had been dropped by the talker before taking his aerial path across the campground.

The two upright men pulled their companions from the fire while furiously slapping at their ignited cohorts. In a few desperate minutes, only smoke surrounded the pair on the ground as their friends looked with shock.

Then they heard thunderous laughter from behind them, causing them to slowly turn and assess Bass. Their curiosity was answered by the business ends of a .45 and .22.

That's when Bass dropped the act. "This darkey may be stupid, but he sure knows better than to make an ass of himself by walkin' up on the backside of an ass. Now if you can get your stuff together, I would appreciate it if you would help your two friends up, and all of you turn around. I have somethin' that will keep your hands occupied for quite a spell."

After securing the four, Bass went through their pockets and retrieved his purse and its contents. He then counted out the money in their pockets and put it in his pocket, after taking out seventy dollars.

He walked into the woods where the informant was hiding and gave him the seventy dollars. It was impossible to tell if the smile on the man's face was from the return of his money or the humor in what he had just observed.

Bass and he both broke out in laughter as they recalled the sight of the four men struggling in the fire, and as they remembered the echo of the mule's bray just before she delivered her thunder.

Bass said, "By the way, the ten dollars I added to your poke is reward for you helping me bring these men to justice. You go home now and take care of your family."

The man was still chuckling as he mounted his pony. Before he turned up the trail and headed for home, he turned and waved to Bass.

With the assistance of Newly and Ed in reading the warrants, Bass and crew soon filled the wagon. By the time they reached Fort Sill, the wagon was overflowing, so they started the long journey back toward Fort Smith. By the time they arrived, they had a string of prisoners walking behind. Several were riding two or even three on horseback, tethered, like a flock of geese to the wagon.

Entering Fort Smith, the group looked like a parade coming to town. There were a total of twenty-six prisoners, several stolen horses and one big dog in the line-up. The city had never seen such a collection of prisoners at one time, and most of the people on the streets could not help but stare as they passed.

Bass could hear people saying, "It looks like Judge Parker is going to have a lot of work."

One of the men on the street rushed out and shook Pete's hand after recognizing one of the prisoners. "Thanks for bringin' that no good thief in. He has been stealin' stuff from all of my friends for years," he told Pete. "I hope they send him away for a long time."

Pete smiled and said, "You shook the wrong hand, friend. I'd be proud to introduce you to the new lawman in the area, Bass Reeves," as he pointed to Bass.

The man hesitated for a moment. He then walked over to Bass and said, "I'd a never thought it, but if Pete says you is awright, I guess you is awright." He paused for a moment and then said, "Thanks."

The arrival at the prison was on the same order as the street. The real difference was that as they entered, Judge Parker himself was standing and waiting beside the deputies. He had a broad smile on his face, obviously pleased with what he was seeing. And while the Judge walked toward the entourage, he extended his hand and warmly grasped Bass'.

"I am extremely proud of my new lawman and look forward to your report on your first venture into the Territory. I hope that you will be with us for some time. Lord knows that there is plenty of work that needs to be done."

"Well, Judge, it was an interesting trip, and I like the action," Bass said. "I think I will be around for a spell."

Chapter 22

The New Lady

Bass had returned once again to Fort Smith, this time with only an average haul of fourteen desperados. It had been a fairly easy trip, except for the fact that he had been stranded for several days by a torrent of rain.

He made sure his wagon and team were returned to the staging station, and he settled up with his crew. The trip had been profitable, in spite of the slow return and lack of any major action.

While at the staging station, Joseph invited him to bed down there, suggested that Bass looked like he needed some rest. Joseph knew that Bass had been on the road for more than forty days and that rest was something hard to come by on the trail.

Joseph said, "Hear your trip was slowed by a flood. This time of year you can expect all kinds of strange weather. Seems it's either too hot or too wet to get a good run in."

"Well, I figure it's just part of the job," Bass said.

"Anything excitin' on the trip?"

"Dog had a good amount of excitement. You know, he has become as good as another posse man. I was away from camp servin' some warrants when Ed got a little careless. He got too close to Mike Hinkle one night, and Mike jumped 'im. Had 'im in a hell of a fix. Got the restraint chain wrapped around his neck and was choking 'im down.

"Dog has been around long enough to know what should happen, and what shouldn't. He jumped ol' Mike and nearly took his ear off. Course, ol' Mike let Ed go and began screamin' like he was on fire. Took Ed several minutes to get Dog loose of 'im. I really don't think Ed was in too big a hurry to get it done," Bass said with a laugh. "The outcome is that Mike will be a lot easier to recognize from now on. Seems that when you ask someone if they've seen a man with only a right ear and a big scar on his left cheek, they should be more inclined to remember 'im."

The two men shared more laughter before Joseph shared his story about the faithful canine.

"That Dog has really turned into somethin'. Before you left on the trip, one of 'em new deputies came in. I was busy greasin' a wagon. He never said nothin', jest started pickin' stuff up and puttin' it in a pile. Next thing I hear is him a hollerin' for help. Seems Dog thought he was stealin' stuff and had forced the new man in a corner. Had his teeth showin' and was not 'bout to let him move. The poor feller was thinkin' he was 'bout to get ate alive," Joseph recalled.

"I got out from under the wagon and had to catch Dog by the neck to get 'im to let the guy out of the corner. Even then, Dog refused to stop his snarlin'. I'd say you got you a real watch dog there, and you should be extra proud to have 'im around."

Bass nodded his head. "I've worked with 'im some, but I usually leave 'im with the wagon. Ed and Newly have done more to train 'im than I have. They got 'im where he will trail, just in case someone might get loose. I sure haven't got a posse man who can smell out a run-away.

"Speakin' of no ear. The other night I was visitin' with some of the prisoners, and one of 'em kept callin' his buddy Coony. He just had one ear like ol' Mike now, and I asked him why he called 'im Coony? He said that they liked to go coon huntin' and had a pack of real trailers. They really liked to watch the hounds fight 'em coons. One night they had treed a really big he coon and was tryin' to get 'im out of the tree. Nothin' they could do would knock 'im out, so the feller tellin' the story climbed up in the tree to knock that big ol' he coon down. Said the hounds were makin' a ruckus and sure itchin' for a fight.

"Well, he finally knocked that coon loose, and he fell about fifteen feet, but he musta made up his mind he wasn't gonna hit in that pack. So, he landed on Coony's head.

"Well, that coon commenced to fight and claw to stay on his perch, and the hounds were a jumpin' to try to get at 'im. Ol' Coony was a fightin' and scratchin', tryin' to get the coon loose and the dogs were a jumpin' and snappin' all the time. They finally pushed the feller into the creek with the water over his head. He's fightin' to stay afloat, and the coon is fightin' to stay out of the water. The coon finally gets a good grasp on the feller's ear and is holdin' on for dear life. The feller has to either drown or get that coon loose. So, he pushes the coon loose with both hands, and the coon takes his ear as a souvenir of the struggle.

"The feller tellin' the story said the ear was so mangled that when he was lookin' at it, he just pulled his knife out and sliced it off even with the feller's head. Said it looked a lot better that way."

Joseph was laughing all through the story, and when it was over, he slapped his knee and said, "What a great story. Sure wish I'd a been there."

Bass said, "It musta been one excitin' evenin'. Goes to show you that you better be careful when you get your prey in their home ground. Seems the same holds true when you're huntin' man."

After Bass had brushed Blaze and made sure that he was well fed, he said, "Joseph, I need to go to the general store and pick up some more ammunition and some other things. I'll be back in a while. Look after my guns and stuff. I think I will just stroll down the street like a normal man."

The walk was relaxing, a real change for the man who usually spent more than ten hours a day in the saddle. He slowed his pace and watched the normal citizens of Fort Smith go about their daily business.

His mind began to wander, and he tried to visualize the way they lived. He could not picture himself doing the things they did. What did they do for excitement? What kept them from becoming so bored that they just wanted to run away? Maybe they had never had the thrill of the hunt or the challenge of facing an armed man with no idea of what he was about to do.

To Bass, what many called normal life was too mundane. He had grown to thrive on his way, coming to the belief that he would always do what he had chosen as a way of life, until age or a bullet put a halt to it.

He reached the general store, and as he was turning to enter, he ran into a lady leaving with several large bundles in her arms. The collision caused her to drop the packages.

"Pardon me, lady. I shoulda been more careful."

"You sure should have been," she snapped.

Bass immediately stooped down and picked up the packages, and said, "Let me help you. Can I take these to your house for you? They're too big a load for a lady."

When he turned his gaze toward the woman, he was shocked.

There stood a lady dressed in a fine dress, but wearing cowboy boots with two pearl handled pistols strapped to her sides. He immediately recognized her as Belle Starr. He had seen her many times in the courthouse posting bail or visiting one of the prisoners.

"Miss Starr, I am truly sorry for my not lookin' where I was goin'. Let me help you with 'em," Bass repeated.

She looked at him for a while and said, "OK, boy. Carry them to my wagon. Follow me."

Bass followed her and placed the packages in the wagon.

He turned, and before he could speak, Belle Starr said, "Who are you? I have seen you some place before."

"Miss Starr, I'm Bass Reeves. I work for Judge Parker."

"You work for that no good bastard," she said. "He and I don't have much good to say about one another. He continually has my friends hauled in, and I continually bail them out or have to hire lawyers to get them some justice."

"I am sorry for your problems, but the way I see it, you're both doin' what you think is right. And from what I know, you're both gonna keep doin' what you're doin'."

Belle looked at him for a moment, and then smiled as she said, "You know, you're right. I guess it will continue as long as one of us exists."

"By the way," Bass said. "I ain't no boy. I think I am as good a man as there is."

"Well, from what I've heard, you are someone that I think I could learn to like. From all I've heard, you are a fair man and treat people with respect. I have to tell you, as a lady, I have to admire that, even though you are a Negro. I have met many a man who I cannot tolerate because of their lack of manners, and most of them were white. So, in your case, let me just say that you are welcome to Younger's Bend anytime, as long as you come there with no malice in your heart."

"Miss Starr, I couldn't promise you that, 'cause I don't know what malice is."

Belle laughed and slapped him on the shoulder. "What I mean is that your boss continually sends people to harass my friends, and you are welcome if you come as a friend and not as someone sent to bother my friends and customers."

Bass dropped his head and thought for a moment.

"Let's make a deal," Bass said. "I'll come by when I have to, and if you can tell me a reason I shouldn't serve a warrant, I won't. But if you know somethin' I should know, you'll tell me. I know that all of them fellers that come by your place aren't all friends to you, and I'd imagine that some of 'em is just as big a pain to you as they are to the rest of the Territory."

"That sounds like it might just work," Belle said. "I do have a lot of people that come through that I have no allegiance to, and some of them have no right running the country. They show no respect to good people, and they sure don't know how to treat a lady. All of the things I have heard about you makes me believe that you will do what you say."

She held out her hand, and Bass took it in his huge hand. They shook, and Belle said, "Next time you're in my area, come by. I hear you are quite a horse fancier, and I have a couple that I would be proud to show you."

"I'll be more than happy to stop," Bass said. "I hear you have a pretty fine cook workin' there, and I can always use a good meal on the road."

Bass tipped his big black hat and turned toward the general store. He smiled as he walked up the stairs, thinking about his unusual meeting he'd just had. He was eager to test whether he had made a friend, gotten fooled by a wiser person or made a pact with the devil. He figured that only time would tell.

Chapter 23

Missed Opportunity

Bass was feeling somewhat dejected. His run, so far, had been routine. The lack of action made him think even more about a fellow named Bob Dillard that other marshals had been talking about wanting to catch. Bass decided that if there was any way he could get a lead on this Dillard fellow, he would spend whatever efforts were needed getting him to justice. Not only did he seem to be a thorn in the side of the people, there was a nice reward on him.

So far, this trip had only yielded him a few whiskey runners and some horse thieves. While he was in camp, however, one of the horse thieves motioned him over.

"Marshal, I know that this guy Dillard is a pain in your side, and I was a wonderin'. If I could help you corral him, might you say a word to the Judge?'

Bass looked directly at the man and said, "There is no doubt that any help you could give would help you greatly with the Judge. I promise that if we can bring in this feller, the Judge would be more than happy to reduce your sentence or even drop the case. In fact, I will recommend it to him."

"Great then, here is what I know. Dillard has some kind of land deal working with some feller up by Pawnee, and it is some kind of sale where the guy is gonna get hooked. They is supposed to meet up next Saturday and close it out."

"How do you know this?" Bass asked.

"The feller was needin' some big money to get the thing done and went to see my brother, who ain't like me. He's workin' for the bank at Cleveland. My brother told me that this feller borrowed several thousand dollars from the bank, and my brother tried to tell 'im it was a bad deal. But, the feller had the stuff to back the loan and insisted that he knew what he was a doin'. So the bank loaned him the money. He is gonna pick it up on Friday and meet up with Bob Dillard on Saturday at the Last Chance saloon in Pawnee about noon. That is all I know, but I am sure Dillard will be there to pick this guy clean."

"Sounds like a right good chance to get 'im corralled, and I promise that if it works out, I will be helpin' you with the Judge," Bass said.

Bass rushed to Ned and said, "We're gonna have to change our plans. I'm sorry, but you fellers are gonna have to stay here for a few days more. I got a tip that I gotta follow up, and I have to hit the road now to make the connection. You've got plenty of food, and I will try and get back quick with a real prize catch that will make us all proud. Ned, I am gonna take your horse cause Blaze is favorin' his right front leg, and I got to make time. Besides, the rest will do 'im good."

"That is fine with me, you're the boss," Ned said. "And I get more pay the longer we are here, so good luck to you."

Bass said, "Go to town and telegraph Stillwater. Have Heck Thomas meet me at Pawnee. He works the area and I might need his help with this one.

Bass put Ned's horse to the test and covered ground as quickly as possible. He knew that he only had one day to reach Pawnee, so he had to travel as fast as he could.

Finally, he crossed Camp Creek and looked at his watch. He had about fifteen minutes to make it to Pawnee. He knew that if he pushed it, he would be right on time.

Bass entered town at straight up noon and headed directly for the Last Chance. The streets were packed with farmers and cowboys in town for their Saturday shopping. The streets were lined with every imaginable wagon and cart. Women and their children were meandering from store to store, and most people appeared to be in a festive mode. Bass hoped that this festivity would not get in the way of the job he had to accomplish.

Despite his rush, Bass still took time to take Ned's horse to the livery, where he told them to give the horse extra care, that he had earned a rest. Bass then rushed to the saloon.

Bass entered and slowly walked through the gathering of men wetting their whistles, talking and laughing. He found a seat near the back of the establishment and settled in to observe the happenings.

Bass spotted one man in a suit sitting alone, carrying a pouch that he clutched tightly in his lap. He was nervously drinking his whiskey while watching with an apprehensive eye everyone who entered.

At about fifteen minutes past noon, two men entered who obviously did not have on their mind the idea of finding a place at the bar. They immediately walked toward the man in the suit, who stood and shook hands with both. The men all sat down at the table and began talking.

Bass watched them talk, observing their every movement. As they continued, the tall stranger pulled some papers from his pouch and handed them across the table to the man in the suit, who began carefully reading the document. As he turned each page, he nodded his head affirmatively. After some time, he reached across the table and shook the tall stranger's hand, then took the pouch from his lap and began to pass it across the table.

Bass stood at this moment and worked his way through the crowd toward the assemblage. After slowly approaching, he said, "Bob Dillard, you are under arrest for so many crimes that Judge Parker will have to call a special day in his court. Now mister, take the pouch back and get the hell away from here."

Bass read the eyes of the two desperados, immediately sensing that they weren't going to go peacefully. So, he pulled his Colt and hoped that it would dissuade them from any foolish action.

No sooner had he cleared his holster than he heard the barkeeper say, "Freeze right there!"

Bass looked across the room to find himself looking down the end of a double barrel shotgun. While this was happening, the crowd at the bar split like a wedge had been driven through them. Some headed for the door, and others rushed to the other side of the room to get out of the line of fire.

Before Bass could say anything, the barkeep added, "You guys get out of here while I hold this darky in his place."

Dillard and his man immediately rushed to the door and vanished.

As they were leaving, Bass said, "Mister, I am a U.S. Marshal, and you just let one of the most wanted men in the Territory escape. If you will let me, I will show you my badge and identification. I'm sorry I didn't do that before, but you're lettin' 'em get away."

The barkeeper motioned with his shotgun for Bass to approach, while keeping both of the cocked barrels aimed toward his chest.

Bass moved as quickly as he thought safe. He pulled back his coat and showed his badge, while at the same time pulling his identification from his coat pocket.

The barkeeper seemed relieved when he saw the badge, but still took a quick look at the identification Bass had produced.

"Looks good to me," the man finally said. "I'm sorry that I stopped you, but I don't allow no gun play in this place, and it sure looked like there was gonna be some."

"I should a told you when I came in," Bass said.

Bass then turned and rushed to the door. He ran at top speed to the livery stable, where he saddled Ned's horse, mounted and road full speed out the door. He took a guess that the men had gone east, so as soon as he cleared the crowded streets, he put his mount into full speed. After crossing Black Bear Creek, he turned east. He hadn't gone a mile when he heard the crack of a rifle and felt his mount stumble. Bass tried with all his strength to keep the horse's head up, but it was to no avail. The stumble continued, and both he and the horse hit the ground. The horse rolled on his side. When Bass tried to free himself, he found that his leg was wedged under the dying animal.

The fortunate thing was that he could at least pull his Winchester from the boot, and he had the cover provided by his fallen mount to provide some protection for him from the shot that followed.

Bass located the smoke from the second round and was able to see the second man that had accompanied Dillard in the bar. Before Bass could fire, however, a third shot was sent his way, ripping a hole in the shirt on Bass' left shoulder.

Bass collected himself and realized that this was no time for accuracy. This was a time for defense. He sighted in on the area from where the shot had come. Then he rapidly fired and levered the Winchester. His shots were taking great chunks of tree and bark from where the sniper was hiding. As soon as Bass had emptied his rifle, he pulled his left Colt and sent two more rounds toward the tree.

This was all the assault that he intended for the sniper, and it worked. Bass could see the man retreat from his hiding place and run to his horse, mount and in full gallop head northeast toward the open stretch of land that would take him toward Skedee.

Bass had to use all his strength to finally free his leg. Once he had done that, he found that the pain was more than he had anticipated.

He turned toward Pawnee and started his walk back to the livery stable where he would need to get a new mount.

As he walked, some of the pain lessened, and by the time he reached town, he was only slightly limping.

On his journey, all he could think about was how close he had come to making his biggest arrest to date. The event made him even more determined to bring in Bob Dillard. Of course, his determination was intensified knowing that Dillard had tried to assassinate him, and he surely did not take kindly to those actions.

When he got to Pawnee, he was met by Heck Thomas.

Heck said, "Looks like you lost your horse. Did you get Dillard?"

"No, the bastard left a man to pick me off, and all he got done was kill my horse. I really hate that, but even worse I hate that I failed to get either one of 'em."

Heck apologized. "I'm sorry that I didn't get here in time, but I was in Wharton, and by the time I got the word, I just didn't have time to get here. Damn, I hate that. We probably could have taken that snake in and reduced a lot of problems here abouts. Maybe next time?"

Bass said, "Maybe, I sure hope so. But thanks for trying."

Chapter 24

Near the End

Bass was introduced to his new supervisor, James Mershon, a few days before taking his new crew back into the Territory.

Mershon was an interesting man, similar to Bass in that both had served in the Civil War as Confederates who deserted the cause. However, Mershon later joined the Union forces, serving with a Kansas unit until the war was over. His excellent record in the war and the fact that he had received several promotions had influenced Judge Parker to promote him to Chief Marshal.

Before leaving on his latest mission, Bass had received his usual armload of warrants before deciding to take his new crew north to Tahlequah. He had heard that there was a lot of trouble brewing in that area, and he needed to check on the situation. With his many friends in the area, Bass thought that he might be of some assistance in calming the hostility.

His new posse man, Frank Pierce, a duly authorized U.S. Deputy Marshal, was chosen by Bass to go on this tour because of the problems that seemed to be appearing in all the areas, especially in the Cherokee Nation. Frank, like Bass, had been very successful serving in the Cherokee area, and Bass felt his experience might be a great asset.

As they approached Tahlequah, Bass decided to set up camp for use as a staging area for the next several days. His new cook, Jake, was a jovial man and seemed to have a great liking for Dog. In fact, his experience was more than adequate, but the attention he paid to Dog probably was the reason Bass chose him.

On the first morning, Bass suggested that they split up, with Frank heading north to get a pulse on what was happening. Before leaving Fort Smith, Bass had received news that there was to be a court hearing over the Becky Beck murder. He knew that Frank was a friend of the Beck family. Bass was hopeful that Frank, with his knowledge of the Beck family, might be able to work out the hostilities between the Becks and Proctors.

The conflict was an Indian problem, but Bass knew that if the situation got violent, it could spill over into the non-Indian population. If something could be done to calm matters, it would benefit everyone in the area.

Bass rode east, primarily to check on some whiskey peddlers he had heard about. In truth, he also wanted to visit Sam Mankiller and his family. It had been far too long since he had seen them, and he was very curious about how the children were doing.

Bass' trip was quiet and easy — so quiet and easy that it raised suspicions in his mind. He could not remember ever making this trip and not meeting a traveler. The world seemed to have vacated and left him all alone.

He topped the ridge to the Mankiller valley and gave the old cry. He was somewhat startled when he gave the greeting because while once such a routine custom for him, it now seemed strange and unnatural.

He continued down the trail, noticing that there were several horses tied to the corral. He also noticed that no one came out on the porch immediately, as was the custom.

All these things made him slow his descent and pull his Winchester from its boot. He knew that it was never foolish to be too cautious, even in places where you should feel comfortable.

To Bass' relief, Sam finally came out on the porch. However, he had his rifle in his hand, only lowering it and coming down the stairs when he saw that it was Bass.

Bass dismounted, and Sam approached with an uneasy smile on his face. He extended one hand while reaching his other arm, with his rifle, up to grasp Bass firmly around the neck. At the same time, he said, "Bass, it is such a comfort to see you alive and well. Did you come because of the trouble? I was so afraid that you were involved."

"What trouble?" Bass asked.

"I guess that you haven't heard," Sam said. "There was a shootout at the Cherokee school, and a bunch of your guys were killed."

"What guys are you talking about?" Bass asked, now greatly concerned.

"Marshals — I hear that at least seven were killed in some kind of blood bath. A bunch of my people was killed as well."

With a bewildered look on his face, Bass asked, "What the hell happened? Who got killed and why?"

"It was that crazy Proctor trial," Sam said. "There is so much bad blood, so much hate stored up over the years and so much resentment that this thing just seemed to bring it all together. I don't know the whole story, but John Pine just got here and was telling it when you came up.

"On top of that, Little Sam is not home, and I worry that he might have been involved. John Pine was there and says that Little Sam was not at the trial, but you know once somethin' like this starts, it draws in all kinds."

"Do you know where to start lookin' for 'im? We can hit the trail right now."

"No, he's been gone for several days. I just hope he's still out hunting and didn't get involved in the mess," Sam said.

Bass thought for a few moments about what his friend reported before deciding. "If he's not back in a few hours, we should go toward Tahlequah and see if we can locate him," Bass said.

"I don't think he's involved in any of it," Sam reassured himself and Bass. "But, that's probably a good idea. Let's go in the house and get more of the story. Some of the guys just got here, and we were just in there talkin' about the slaughter. John Pine can tell us all about it."

Once inside, there were greetings and introductions, with Lidia refilling coffee cups, before John began again to tell all he had seen and heard. "Well, as I was tellin' you, I jest went cause I knew that there had been so much trouble over whether or not the Cherokee could give Zeke a fair trial. You know that Zeke and lots of the others are members of the Going Snake band, and they're sick and tired of the white men meddlin' in our affairs. I wanted to be a witness to our people doin' the right thing.

"You know, Zeke always said that he shot Becky Beck by accident. Sure, he admitted to shootin' her husband or boyfriend — whatever he was. But his trial weren't 'bout that.

"They moved the trial to the Whitmore School, just out of town. The school was chose 'cause it had so few windows, and they felt it would be easier to protect the people inside and keep out the people they didn't want around. Sounded like a good idea to me.

"When the trial started, I couldn't get in 'cause there were so many people. So, I was standin' on the front porch, but I could see in the door 'cause they left it open for some air to get in.

"Judge Sixkiller had jest started the trial when a bunch of guys came ridin' up. They was all totin' iron, and most of 'em had shotguns. I knew right then and there that trouble was gonna happen, especially when I seen that most of 'em was Becks or friends of the Beck family.

"As they was a gettin' off their horses, one of them Becks started swingin' his shotgun and walkin' straight to the door. I got out of the way, but there were four armed men on the porch that was supposed to keep others out.

"Well, Beck said, 'We is the law, duly deputized to come and see that Zeke gets what's comin' to 'im, and if he don't, we has got a writ to take 'im back to Fort Smith and let the white men's law take care of it.'

"Jest as soon as he said that, you could hear folks inside hollerin' for Beck to get the hell out of there. In general, what they was sayin' was that this was a Cherokee problem, and the Cherokees had the rights to pass judgment on Zeke, and no federal law could.

"Beck kept on a comin' and pushed his way past the guards. When he got inside, he didn't even stop to try and figure out what was takin' place. He jest raised his shotgun and started aimin' it toward Zeke. Before he could pull the trigger, Zeke's brother grabbed the barrel and pulled it to the side. I guess he pulled it too hard, 'cause it went off right into his chest. Blood and stuff flew out of his back and all over people. Of course, he let the barrel go, and it seemed to not even slow Beck down. He turned the shotgun back toward Zeke and pulled the trigger. Hit Zeke in the leg as he was jumpin' toward one of the guards and pulled the guard's pistol right out a his hand.

"Zeke commenced to fire back toward Beck, and it seems like everyone in the room produced an iron and started a firin'.

"Beck fell where he stood, and some of the guys ran to the door and was greeted by all kinds of shootin' from them marshals.

"Well, I hit the ground and crawled around to the side of the school as fast as I could. All the time I was crawlin' there was continual firin'. I don't know how long it went on, but I bet it was at least fifteen minutes. I peeked around the corner a time or two, and I seen some of them marshals and some others mount up and leave nothin' but dust. But some of them had no choice — their horses had spooked, and they was afoot.

"They stood their ground and put up one hell of a fight, but they all hit the ground sooner or later. When the last one fell, the shootin' stopped, and the screamin' started.

"There were people everywhere. Two of the marshals were lyin' right at the steps. One of 'em, I think his name was Owens, got in the house across the street, and the widow that lives there took 'im in and wouldn't let nobody come in after 'im. After a while, she had 'em bring in several wounded and started fixin' on 'em. It was quite a sight. All those that had been a fightin' each other was now layin' out on the floor together.

"I guess that old widow lady must a had some kind of sympathy pains, 'cause she made some fellers hitch up her wagon and go pick up all of the bodies and bring 'em to her porch and lay 'em all out in the shade in some kinda comfortin' way.

"There were ten bodies a lyin' there. Three of 'em was Cherokees, and the others were marshals. One of 'em dead was Lawyer Alberty, Zeke's defense lawyer. Judge Sixkiller also was hit, but looked like it twernt nothin' to get excited about. Before I left, I checked in the house again, and there was a passel of hurt fellers in there. Most of 'em looked like they'd make it. Marshal Owens, though, looked awful bad.

"You know the thing about Owens is that both the Becks and the Proctors like that guy, and, as far as I know, most all the Cherokees like 'im too. Maybe that's why they had sent 'im, hopin' for some kinda peaceful settlement to the thing. Seems the problem is that they let them Becks come as marshal and they should a known that them Proctors weren't gonna stand for that."

The room was in complete silence after John finished talking.

Bass broke the silence. "My Lord, what a tragedy. I know Owens — rode with 'im a time or two. A good man, a really good man. I hope he makes it. Now I understand why the trail was so empty and nothin' was movin'. This Going Snake thing will probably be the worst day that the marshal service 'll ever have. At least I hope so."

Several other opinions were expressed, and it was decided that whatever happened, it was going to do nothing but bring more bad blood into the Cherokee Nation.

Before leaving, the men all promised that they would try to preach calm and peace to whomever they met, and they hoped that they could diffuse all the hostility that was going to exist.

As the men were departing one direction, Little Sam was spotted coming down the trail. Sam, Lidia and Bass all ran out and happily greeted him. The young man seemed to enjoy the greetings, but was puzzled by the enthusiasm. However, after hearing about the events at Whitmore School, he better understood the concern.

"That sounds unbelievable," Little Sam said. "It's hard to understand why there's not some way of stopping this ongoing feud. I know that it goes clear back to the sell-off of our people's land back in the East and has carried over into continual disputes between the survivors of those people, but we have to learn that if we want to survive as a tribe, that we must unify. We have enough enemies on the outside. We could use a little peace and harmony amongst us."

"Spoken like an educated man," Bass said, admiring the young man he had known since he was a young boy. "It makes me wonder if I had anythin' to do with your raisin'."

"Bass, the things you taught me were what made me become an educated man," Little Sam said. "It wasn't the use of the gun that made me. It was your teaching me to stay with something and work hard at improvement that I was never to take shortcuts, and to do my tasks before the day is done. These are the things you taught me, and I will never forget it. Thanks to you, I think I'm going to become a lawyer."

"Well, maybe someday I'll bring you a bunch of clients," Bass said with a smile.

"Sounds like a deal," Sam said, continuing the good-natured exchange.

Bass then turned his attention to the other Mankiller he had loved since she was a small girl. "Tell me now, how is Sarah, and where is she?"

"She is still away," Lidia said. "But she is now teaching in a school that they have set up in Pennsylvania that is only for Indians. She loves it, but should be home for Christmas. It would be great if you and Jennie and the kids could come for Christmas."

"It would take one of my prisoner wagons to get that done. You know I now got eight kids, and they are a passel of energy. I think that is why I stay on the road. However, I thank you for the invite, and if there is some way we can work it out, we'll sure ponder on it."

"How are the kids doing?" Lidia asked.

"Well, the girls are doin' great. Their schoolin' is goin' well, and they are a real joy. The boys are another thing. They're typical boys, always up to somethin', but I have plenty of work for 'em and try to keep 'em in line. I think maybe me bein' gone so much might have somethin' to do with the trouble they get in."

Lidia said, "Let's go in the house and have some coffee. I know you could use it."

"I sure could, but I need to get back on the trail soon. I have to see what's happenin', and my posse man is over by Tahlequah and might be needin' my help."

Chapter 25

Close Call

Marshal Mershon met Bass as he was preparing to leave for his next run through the Territory. The marshal motioned for Bass to come into his office, where he said, "Bass, I have a special assignment for you. I know you have already had one run in with Bob Dillard, and I just wanted you to know that we need to get him as soon as possible. I feel that you have the best opportunity to complete this task.

"This feller is really causin' a lot of trouble, and, as you know, he is slippery as axle grease. Why he ever changed from a prosperous farmer and rancher, we don't know. But, he sure has been good at his new occupation — too good. So, if you get any lead on him, drop everything else and take him down any way you can," Marshal Mershon said, looking Bass straight in the eye.

"This feller moves like the wind and seems to have no set pattern to what he wants to get involved with. He has robbed banks, stagecoaches, trains, individuals, and stores. He has been involved in cattle stealin' and horse rustlin'. We know that he has a gang that he can call on at anytime, but moves so fast and in so many directions that he just seems to be anywhere and everywhere that my guys ain't," the marshal complained.

Bass said, "He owes me, and I'll get him if possible. I've no kindness for folks that try to bushwhack me."

"Well he has been a pain in my ass long enough. If you get a chance, take him out anyway possible." the marshal said, mincing no words.

"I'll keep an ear to the ground on all of my runs from now on," Bass promised.

***

Bass had an arm full of warrants, so many it seemed more than a person would want to undertake. However, the story of Bob Dillard heightened his interest. If there was one thing that Bass loved, it was a challenge. The fact that others had failed pricked his interest.

On this trip, his first major stop was Wagoner. He was lucky that on the first day there, he located and arrested two of the men on his list. He secured them in the prison wagon before going back to ask around for some of the others. This could be a quick and prosperous trip if his luck continued.

He would ask several people if they knew people in his warrant bundle, but seldom got positive responses. It was just like Pistol Pete had said — unless they needed your help, you were not going to get much from the citizens. They mostly operated on the notion that if it did not concern them, then it was best to stay out of it.

Bass' travels took him down the road, and over the next several days, he was successful in finding four of those on the warrants.

Now headed toward the Seminole Nation, Bass stopped at one of his old friend's homesteads and visited for a while. He always made it a habit to continue his friendships, especially since they had proven to be his best source of information, often shortening his searches.

Bass dismounted before a man named Gilbert Franklin, a friend of Bass' deceased love, Jane, and a person who in the past had given him valuable information.

"Gilbert, how are you, and how's the family?" Bass asked.

"Bass, my friend, I'm glad to see you. It has been far too long," Gilbert said.

"Well, you're lookin' fit, and I reckon that your leg is mended from that horse throwin' you. You sure were a hobblin' last time I was by," Bass said.

"Yea, I was a might stoved up at the time, but my wife got me back in shape. She had to, or else she'd had to do all the work," the man said with a laugh.

"As usual, I'm wondering, Gilbert, if you've heard of any lawbreakers about. I'm especially lookin' for a guy named Dillard, but I have a passle of warrants, and if'n you can give me a lead, I would be appreciatin' it."

"Bob Dillard," Gilbert said, knowingly. "Yep, I know the feller, but he ain't been in these parts for a spell. I did hear from a neighbor that there is two white men and two Negroes a sellin' a bunch of whiskey over by Wewoka. They is a workin' in the open, and if'n you get over there, they should be easy pickin's."

"I thank you for that piece of information. Think I'll just head that way now. But if you or your neighbors hear of this Dillard feller, let me know. You can send a telegraph to headquarters in Fort Smith, and they will get me the word. By the way, there is a bounty on this feller, and I will be glad to share it with any of you that gives me a hand."

Bass tipped his hat before mounting to continue his trip. He did not mind changing his course toward Wewoka. There was always someone, someplace that needed his services, and all he cared about was filling his wagon.

The day was getting long when he turned the bend in the road and saw two men standing under a tree, apparently resting their horses. As he approached, he recognized them as two of the Brunter brothers. He had warrants for all of the brothers, and their reputations as thieves and rustlers had kept them on his list for several months.

He dismounted, reached in his saddlebag for his warrants and walked toward the two. He knew they recognized him and was expecting trouble from them at any minute. But this time, he was fooled with an unusual circumstance.

There were only two horses and two men. Therefore, he had assumed that they were the only ones in the area. But as Bass approached, a third brother came out from behind a thicket with his pistol in hand and cocked.

"You black bastard, we knows you, and 'ave been runnin' from you for over a month now. Looks like our runnin' is 'bout to stop," the man said with an evil smile on his face.

Bass acted like he didn't hear the words. He just kept fumbling with the papers in his hand.

"You're the Brunter boys, ain't you?" he asked.

"You know good and well we is," the brother with the gun drawn said.

"Well, I want you to take a look at these here papers and make sure that your names is right. I sure don't want to make any mistakes and bring in the wrong fellers."

"What the hell is you talkin' about?" the man asked. "We is gonna kill you, here and now."

"Well 'fore you do, have a look see," Bass said, holding forth the papers. One of the brothers automatically reached for them, but just before his hand grasped the extended papers, Bass dropped them. The wind grabbed them and sent them scattering. Instinctively, all eyes looked down.

That was all the edge Bass needed. He cleared his holster with his right hand, and as he swung his Colt clear of its encasement, he pulled the trigger.

The shot hit the brother with the gun in the middle of his forehead, and he fell like a giant oak tree.

The brother standing closest to Bass reached for his pistol and was just clearing his holster when Bass slapped his huge left hand around the man's gun hand and forcefully pushed the pistol back in the holster.

Bass tightened his grip and pushed harder to keep the pistol from escaping its confine.

The brother now reached his left hand across and was trying with all of his strength to free his weapon, but Bass kept his grip on the weapon. He also kept his captive between himself and the other brother, who had now cleared his weapon and was trying to get a clear shot at Bass.

Bass continued to maneuver the struggling brother into a position where his pistol-wheeling brother couldn't get a clear shot at Bass. It became like a dance of death as one man tried to shoot Bass, while Bass kept the other brother as a human shield.

The struggle lasted for several seconds, until Bass was able to push the struggling brother aside and fire his .45, hitting the other brother with great accuracy. The remaining brother made an attempt to grab Bass' other gun. Bass seemed to know what the man was going to do, even before the man made his play. With all of his force, Bass slashed the gun he was holding into the head of the sole surviving brother, connecting solidly with the man's temple.

The brother's knees crumpled, and he hit the ground with such force that the air could be heard rushing from his body.

Bass stood with his pistol in hand and surveyed the area. He knew that the first brother was definitely dead. Slowly, he approached the other brother he had shot. There was no sign of movement as Bass kicked the man's pistol away from his hand and with his foot turned him over. He really did not have to turn him over, as he could see a gaping hole in his back where the slug had exited his body. Bass was just making sure that he would never again have to worry about another surprise visit from this brother.

Bass returned to manacle the clubbed brother. As he was securing the man's hands, he noticed that there was no sign of breathing coming from him.

Bass rolled him over and found that the man's eyes were hollow. Bass had seen this too many times. He knew that there was no reason to manacle the man. His pistol's force had guaranteed the last brother would never bother anyone again.

Bass stood for a moment and observed his day's work. Here were three brothers, none of whom had earned a reason for mercy, but for some reason Bass just hoped that he had done the Lord's work. After some thought, he consoled himself by replaying the events. He realized that the men had held every advantage from the time Bass arrived. Yet, he had triumphed. Therefore, he told himself, it must have been God's will that he had fulfilled. His preacher must be right in that God had given him the use of the sword to protect those who were not able to protect themselves.

Bass strapped the three men on the two horses, before heading to Wewoka. As he entered the town, people stopped to stare at him and his load, and several people followed the procession to the sheriff's office.

The sheriff saw Bass coming, so he stepped out of his office to greet the returning lawman. Then he walked to the horses and turned up the heads of each of the dead men, looking at their faces.

"Bass, looks like you've taken out all the Brunters in one day. I'd a never thought it, but I sure is relieved," the sheriff said. "These low down critters has been the cause of more problems in these here parts than one could rightly imagine. You know, you should be proud. I can't prove it, but I sure do think that they is the ones that kilt Marvin McDonald and his family. Shot Marvin, and raped and kilt his wife and daughter. It was one really awful sight. Course, we know they has been runnin' amuck for months now."

"I was just doin' my job. But Sheriff, I want you to know that there was one time this day that I wondered if I might not be the one strapped to a horse," Bass said, shaking his head in wonder and gratitude.

As they conversed, a crowd gathered. People walked around the bodies secured to the horses and took turns looking into the faces of the once dreaded scalawags. Most of the spectators expressed relief that the villains could no longer prey on the good people of the land.

While the crowd looked, the town photographer pushed his way through the gathering with his bulky equipment and asked if anyone would help get the bodies down so he could get a picture of the fallen men.

Several men stepped forward, and after the photographer promised he would take their picture if they helped, the volunteers eagerly untied the corpses and lifted them to the boardwalk. They then propped the dead men up against the wall of the sheriff's office.

After struggling to get the slain men sitting just right, the photographer finally got them into the position he wanted and stepped back to set up his equipment. The fuss he went through to get his camera arranged and his flash loaded drew as much attention as the corpses had in the beginning.

Finally, he was prepared and slid under the black cloth of the camera. In a moment, the pan he was holding ignited, and a flash brighter than any muzzle fire lit the area. The blinding flash drew moans and gasps, then applause from the by-standers.

Bass' awareness was drawn to the crowd by the flash, and he stood in amazement at how much attention and entertainment he had brought to the town.

After just a few seconds, Bass returned to business. "Sheriff, I need to telegraph Fort Smith, and tell 'em that I've turned the Brunter brothers' bodies over to you, and I'm goin' on about my work. Do you have a office here?"

The sheriff said, "Yep, jest go on down the street yonder, and you'll see the railroad station. The feller in there is Idas, and he'll help yah."

Bass mounted and headed directly to the station where he rode straight to the window. Staying in the saddle, he soon was staring down into Idas' eyes.

Idas said, "Hey, I know you. We met in Belle Starrs' place a while back."

"That's sure right. How you been?" Bass asked, recognizing the man.

"Well, I got this here job, and things has been goin' along pretty well. So, I got no complaints. What can I do for you, Marshal?"

"I need to send a telegraph to Fort Smith and tell 'em that I got the Brunter brothers. Could you do that for me? Tell 'em they're dead, and I have left their bodies with the sheriff."

"Be more than happy to. Wait jest a minute."

Bass stayed in the saddle, surveying the area as the telegraph tapped away. It seemed that no sooner had the message been sent than the tapping began again. Idas started writing, then turned and looked up at Bass.

"Seems they been lookin' for you. They say that Bob Dillard has been seen, as of yesterday over by Fort Gibson. They advise you to get there as fast as you can."

"Well, that is jest the kind of news I've been waitin' for. I had planned on goin' home for a spell, but there is too much money on that man's head to pass up a chance to bring 'im in. Besides that he created a situation that he personally owes me for. So, I thank you for the information, and I'll be goin' now."

The End

10/1/24

Printed in Great Britain
by Amazon

35903858R00089